Matthew Russell

Sonnets On The Sonnet: An Anthology

Matthew Russell

Sonnets On The Sonnet: An Anthology

ISBN/EAN: 9783741100246

Manufactured in Europe, USA, Canada, Australia, Japa

Cover: Foto ©Thomas Meinert / pixelio.de

Manufactured and distributed by brebook publishing software (www.brebook.com)

Matthew Russell

Sonnets On The Sonnet: An Anthology

Sonnets on the Sonnet

AN ANTHOLOGY

COMPILED BY THE

REV. MATTHEW RUSSELL, S.J.

> 'Tush! none but minstrels like of sonneting'
> *Love's Labour Lost*, Act iv. Scene 3

LONGMANS, GREEN, AND CO.
39 PATERNOSTER ROW, LONDON
NEW YORK AND BOMBAY
1898

All rights reserved

DEDICATION

Within this booklet nought shall have a place
   Save sonnets with the Sonnet for their theme;
   'Tis fitting, therefore, that its front should gleam
With some bright name of subtlest power and grace
In sonnet-craft—not chosen from the race
   Of bygone poets, for 'tis wrong, I deem,
   Back o'er past ages wistfully to dream,
As if the Present were too dull and base.

All ages have their poets, and our day
   Can bravely hold its own 'gainst any other
     In this poetic form that poets cherish.
The poet's poet-wife has passed away;
   Christina, too, great almost as her brother—
     But Alice Meynell's sonnets shall not perish.

                                 M. R.

DISTRIBUTION

Two models here have sat for all the rest,
   Or nearly all.   De Vega's quaint design
   Shows you the Sonnet building line on line
Till in its perfect form it stands confessed.
Wordsworth with cunning words its worth expressed
   And its true modest dignity defined,
   While he the names of all the six entwined
Who till his day had woven sonnets best.

These twain hath aped full many a sonneteer :
   First, in these pages Lope's copyists throng,
   Next, Wordsworth and his faithful echoes come;
And then the Sonnet's functions are made clear.
   Of other self-describing forms of song
   Our last few leaves will kindly shelter some.

PREFACE

THIS collection contains a hundred and fifty-seven sonnets, the subject of each of which is the Sonnet itself regarded from some point of view. A hundred and twenty-four of these are English, gathered from books and journals published in England, Ireland, and the United States. From French poets we have taken twenty-three sonnets, from German five, from Italian three, and from Spanish two. But these last two are the earliest of all our samples. We have not discovered any in early Italian literature.

Besides translations of many of the foreign sonnets, the compiler and his friends have contributed the whole of the fourth division of this book. Several years ago the subject was introduced to the readers of the 'Irish Monthly,' which is edited by the compiler of this volume. Questions and answers on the subject appeared also in 'Notes and Queries.' These premature announcements brought assistance from many correspondents on both sides of the Atlantic. One of the most generous of these helpers, MR. E. B. BROWNLOW, of Montreal, Canada, has already passed away. He died September 8, 1895. His 'Orpheus and other Poems' was published by his friends at Montreal since his death.

PREFACE

The first division of our book begins with the famous sonnets of Lope de Vega and Hurtado de Mendoza, describing humorously the mechanism of a sonnet; and with these are grouped some thirty other sonnets that deal with the physical structure of this peculiar species of poem.

The second part places in front that sonnet of Wordsworth which speaks of 'the sonnet's scanty plot of ground'; and this is followed by more than fifty others treating of the nature and objects of the sonnet.

The third part takes its note from another celebrated sonnet of Wordsworth, 'Scorn not the sonnet,' which mentions some of the great masters of this form of poetical composition; and with it are associated thirty that do likewise.

Part IV., under the title of 'The Sonnet's latest Votaries,' gives some thirty 'sonnets on the sonnet' which were written expressly with a view to this compilation.

Part V. is a sort of appendix, in which what has been done for the sonnet is done, generally by a single example, for rondeau, villanelle, roundel, ballade, triolet, and quatrain, and also for the classical metres, hexameter, anapæst, &c.

Another appendix puts together a great many pithy statements by many writers, generally of high authority, about the nature, functions, and structure of the sonnet; and a postscript directs the attention of the student to certain sonnet-articles.

Permission to make this use of their writings has been most kindly given by MR. THEODORE WATTS-DUNTON, MR. SWINBURNE, MR. AUSTIN DOBSON, MR. WALTER E. HENLEY, MR. WILFRID BLUNT,

PREFACE

ARCHBISHOP ALEXANDER, REV. PROFESSOR W. W. SKEAT, and also by the Editor of 'The Spectator' for sonnets which appeared in that journal. I crave forgiveness from the owner of any copyright poem quoted here with whom I may have failed to communicate.

MR. ADDINGTON SYMONDS, who has since died, wrote as follows from Venice on April 27, 1892 :—

'I have received your note here to-day, and reply that I shall be glad to see my three Sonnets on the Sonnet reprinted in your book. Only, I must make one condition, that I should see the proofs. A good many poems by me have got into hymn-books and anthologies, and have suffered greatly from careless editing.'

MR. R. WATSON GILDER, MR. ANTONY MOREHEAD, MRS. JULIA DORR, and MISS EDITH THOMAS will be recognised as Americans. MR. S. V. COLE dates from Williamstown, Massachusetts, and MRS. HARRIET ROBINSON from Malden in the same State. MR. SHOEMAKER's sonnets appeared in 'The Literary World' of New York in the years 1879–1883.

The French sonneteers, except two or three well-known names, have been found in the 'Almanach du Sonnet,' published annually as the organ of an Académie du Sonnet which was founded at Aix, in Provence, in the year 1874. I have the volumes for four years after that date, but I do not know how long it lasted, or if it survives. Perhaps one of the members of this Academy of the Sonnet was M. LUDOVIC SARLAT, who died last year in Dordogne, aged 82, leaving after him in print sixteen hundred and seventeen sonnets.

In our collection of Sonnets on the Sonnet, some omissions will, of course, be detected. But let it be

PREFACE

noted that such pieces as Thomas Hood's 'Sonnet on a Sonnet' have been purposely left out as not coming within our scope; for these are written in answer to other particular sonnets, and regard the matter of the individual sonnet in question, not the matter or form of the sonnet itself considered as a peculiar species of poetical composition. Some, indeed, that would properly belong to our plan, have remained undiscovered, though mentioned by certain authors. Thus, Italian friends, and the readers of 'Notes and Queries,' have sought in vain for an Italian sonnet on the sonnet by Marino, alluded to by Mr. Samuel Waddington in his 'Sonnets of Europe,' on the authority of Lord Holland. A similar sonnet by Nencioni, referred to by Carducci, and a French one by Poupo, mentioned in the 'Almanach du Sonnet,' have also escaped the most diligent search.

However, sins of omission are not the worst; and our readers are hardly likely to complain of our sonnets for being too few, as *we* may have to complain of our readers.

M. R.

CONTENTS

	PAGE
DEDICATION	v
DISTRIBUTION	vi
PREFACE	vii

I. THE STRUCTURE OF THE SONNET
Text from Boileau, p. 2

THE EARLIEST 'SONETO DEL SONETO'	*Hurtado de Mendoza*	3
THE SAME TRANSLATED	*The Editor*	3
THE SECOND SPANISH SONNET ON THE SONNET	*Lope de Vega*	4
THE SAME TRANSLATED	*J. P. Collier*	4
ANOTHER TRANSLATION	*James Young Gibson*	5
THE SAME TRANSLATED INTO FRENCH	*Régnier Desmarais*	5
AN ENGLISH TRAVESTY	*Thomas Edwards*	6
ON THE STRUCTURE OF THE SONNET	*Anna Seward*	6
THE AGILE SONNETEER	*Antony Morehead*	7
AN AMERICAN SONNET ON THE SONNET	*Edith Thomas*	7
THE SHAKSPERIAN SONNET	*Archbishop Alexander*	8
THE PETRARCHAN SONNET	*The Same*	8
SONNETEERING UNDER DIFFICULTIES	*Bishop Fitzgerald*	9
QUATRAINS AND TERCETS	*George A. Greene*	9
LE SONNET	*Théophile Gautier*	10
THE SAME TRANSLATED	*D. Moncrieff O'Connor*	10

CONTENTS

		PAGE
A SECOND FRENCH SONNET ON THE SONNET	*Louis Veuillot*	11
UN AUTRE	*Henri Meilhac*	11
DAS SONETT	*Augustus W. Schlegel*	12
THE SAME TRANSLATED	*The Editor*	12
ANOTHER GERMAN SONNET ON THE SONNET	*Daniel Schiebeler*	13
A THIRD GERMAN SONNET ON THE SONNET	*Otto von Loeben*	13
AN ITALIAN SONNET ON THE SONNET	*Anon.*	14
TO A SCOTCH TYRO	*Rev. J. J. Judkin*	14
WHAT IS A SONNET?	*M. Montagu*	15
ANOTHER ANSWER TO THE SAME QUESTION	*Anon.*	15
AND ANOTHER	*Anon.*	16
RIVAL SONNETEERS	*John Adamson*	16
THE SONNET SONNETISED	*Harriet H. Robinson*	17
SONNET IN A CONCERT ROOM	*Sir William Rowan Hamilton*	17
EVERY MAN HIS OWN POET	'*The Chicago Tribune*'	18
A BOOK OF SONNETS	*Anon.*	18
SONNET EN BOUTS-RIMÉS	*De la Motte*	19
SONNET TO A REJECTED SONNET	*W. E. Gladstone*	19
DON'T!	'*Daily News*'	20
WOMAN AND THE SONNET	*A. M. F. Robinson*	20

II. THE NATURE OF THE SONNET

Text from J. R. Lowell, p. 22

'THE SONNET'S SCANTY PLOT OF GROUND'	*Wordsworth*	23
ON THE PECULIAR CHARACTER OF THE SONNET	*Anna Seward*	23
A SONNET IS A SONNET	*Capel Lofft*	24
RECANTATION	*Kirke White*	24
FLOWERY CHAINS	*Keats*	25
A MOMENT'S MONUMENT	*Dante Rossetti*	25
OH! FOR A PERFECT SONNET	*Wilfrid Blunt*	26
THE SONNET'S VOICE	*Theodore Watts-Dunton*	26
ON READING THE PRECEDING SONNET	*William Bell Scott*	27
THE SONNET'S TWO VOICES	*J. K. Stephen*	27
WHAT IS THE SONNET?	*Herbert New*	28

CONTENTS

		PAGE
SONNET-WRITING	Father Faber	28
ON RECEIVING MAIN'S 'TREASURY OF SONNETS'	Perry	29
THREE SONNETS ON THE SONNET	John Addington Symonds	29
THREE MORE SONNETS ON THE SONNET	I. P. Deane	31
THE SONNETEER LIMITED	Edward S. Creamer	32
ORIGIN OF THE SONNET	Thomas Noble	33
SONNET IN MEMORY OF A SONNET-WRITER	R. W. Gilder	33
TO A CRITIC	Mrs. Julia Dorr	34
TO A POET	The Same	34
A DIALOGUE ON THE SONNET	Thomas Auld	35
SONNET PAUSES	The Same	35
A SONNET SIMILE	The Same	36
THE SONNET'S GOLDEN CASKET	Ferdinand E. Kappey	36
THE SACREDNESS OF THE SONNET	James Edmeston	37
A CAUTION TO SONNETEERS	Elliot Stock	37
THE SONNET'S DIGNITY	Allen Upward	38
TERZA RIMA AND THE SONNET	James Haskin	38
A HIDDEN ACROSTIC	Edgar Allan Poe	39
MULTUM IN PARVO	James Cochrane	39
COMMUNIA PROPRIE	Anon.	40
FROM THE GREAT DEEP	S. V. Cole	40
TWO SONNETS ON THE SONNET	W. L. Shoemaker	41
DAS SONETT	Goethe	42
THE SAME TRANSLATED	Rev. George O'Neill, S.J.	42
MÊME AVEC CENT DÉFAUTS	Louis Veuillot	43
'UN SONNET SANS DÉFAUT'	Ernest Lacoste	43
SONNET CONTRE LE SONNET	Th. Richard-Baudin	44
BOILEAU AGAIN	Léon Magnier	44
LE SONNET	The Same	45
LE SONNET EST LIMOUSIN	Abbé Joseph Roux	45
A TAILOR-MADE JACKET	Joséphin Soulary	46
'UT PICTURA POESIS'	Georges Garnier	46
THE SONNET-IN-LAW	G. Hipp	47
POURQUOI DES SONNETS?	A. Boursault	47
LE SONNET ET LE SIÈCLE	Auguste de Vaucelle	48
SONNETTISTES À L'ŒUVRE	J. B. Gaut	48
AL SONETTO	G. Prati	49

CONTENTS

		PAGE
THE SONNET OF A SEPTUAGENARIAN	*William Mason*	49
SONNET-GOLD	*Eugene Lee-Hamilton*	50

III. THE MASTERS OF THE SONNET
Text from Andrew Lang, p. 52

SCORN NOT THE SONNET	*Wordsworth*	53
THE SAME IMITATED IN FRENCH	*Sainte-Beuve*	53
THE SAME PARODIED AT NEW YORK	*Anon.*	54
THE SAME SUPPLEMENTED	*Archdeacon Bayley*	54
SCORN IT IF YOU WILL!	*Francis Heywood Warden*	55
TOY OF THE TITANS!	*Ebenezer Elliot*	55
THE POWERS OF THE SONNET	*Ebenezer Elliot*	56
TO T. B. ALDRICH ON HIS SONNETS	*W. L. Shoemaker*	56
THE TREASURE BARK	*W. L. Shoemaker*	58
A GOLDEN CLIMAX	*John Charles Earle*	58
APOLOGY FOR TRANSLATING PETRARCH	*Charles Tomlinson*	59
THE MASTERS	*Francis P. McKeon*	59
WHAT IS A SONNET?	*Eugene Lee-Hamilton*	60
ANOTHER ANSWER TO THE SAME QUESTION	*R. W. Gilder*	60
WRITTEN ON A BLANK LEAF IN MR. S. WADDINGTON'S 'SONNETS OF EUROPE'	*Thomas Auld*	61
ELIXIR	*Edith Wharton*	61
TO PETRARCH	*Auguste Brizeux*	62
THE SAME IMITATED	*Rev. George O'Neill, S.J.*	62
A GERMAN SONNET ON THE SONNET	*Augustus von Platen*	63
THE SAME TRANSLATED	*The Editor*	63
IL SONETTO	*Carducci*	64
THE SAME TRANSLATED	*Charlotte G. O'Brien*	64
AL SONETTO	*Carducci*	65
THE SAME TRANSLATED	*Charlotte G. O'Brien*	65
ANOTHER VERSION OF THE SAME	*E. B. Brownlow*	66
A JOSÉPHIN SOULARY	*Prosper Blanchemain*	66
THE ACADEMY OF THE SONNET	*Comte Lafond*	67
FRENCH MASTERS	*Irma Méray*	67
A EVARISTE BOULAY-PATY	*Alfred de Vigny*	68
THE SAME TRANSLATED	*Rev. George O'Neill, S.J.*	68

CONTENTS

IV. THE SONNET'S LATEST VOTARIES
Text from Lowell's 'Fable for the Critics,' p. 70

		PAGE
A SONNET ON THE SONNET . .	*Rev. Mosse Macdonald*	71
THROUGH THE LATTICE	*Elinor Sweetman*	71
A WOMAN'S SONNET	'*M. E. Francis*'	72
A FATHER'S SONNET	*Count Plunkett*	72
SOUL AND BODY	*Frederick C. Kolbe, D.D.*	73
ROS IN ROSA	*Alice F. Barry*	73
A WILLING SLAVE	*Charles F. Forshaw, LL.D.*	74
A SET OF SIMILES . . .	*Edward Burrough Brownlow*	74
THE ONENESS OF THE SONNET	*Denis Moncrieff O'Connor*	75
THE SONNET OF A LIFETIME . .	*John Kane, LL.D.*	75
THE LAWS OF THE SONNET .	*R. E. Egerton-Warburton*	76
THE SONNET'S SOLACE . .	*Charlotte Grace O'Brien*	76
THE COMPLETE SONNETEER . . .	*John E. Norcross*	77
SONNETS BY RULE	*The Same*	77
THE SONNET	*T. H. Wright*	78
THE DRY BONES OF A SONNET . . .	*The Editor*	78
SONNET LAWS SELF-EXPOUNDED . . .	*The Same*	79
SONNET MECHANISM	*The Same*	79
A HUNDREDTH DEFENCE OF THE SONNET .	*The Same*	80
A TYPEWRITER'S SONNET	*The Same*	80
A MAGAZINE OF SONNETS	*The Same*	81
'SO EASY NOT TO WRITE' . . .	*The Same*	81
SOLATIOLUM	*The Same*	82
AN OLD MAN'S SONNET	*The Same*	82
A JEWELLED SHRINE . . .	*Rev. Joseph Keating, S.J.*	83
SONNETS OF LIFE:—		
I. YOUTH		83
II. AGE		84
III. L'ENVOI	*Rev. Hugh T. Henry*	84

CONTENTS

V. THE SONNET'S KINDRED SELF-DESCRIBED
Text from George Macdonald, p. 86

		PAGE
A RONDEAU ON THE RONDEAU	*Voiture*	87
THE SAME IMITATED	*Austin Dobson*	87
MY FIRST RONDEAU	*The Editor*	88
MY LAST RONDEAU	*The Same*	88
THE RONDEAU	*E. B. Brownlow*	89
AN UNPUNCTUATED VILLANELLE	*H. M. B.*	89
A VILLANELLE ON THE VILLANELLE	*W. E. Henley*	90
HOW TO COMPOSE A VILLANELLE	*Rev. Walter Skeat*	91
POUR FAIRE UNE VILLANELLE	*Joseph Boulmier*	91
THE SAME TRANSLATED	*James Bowker*	92
HOW A ROUNDEL IS WROUGHT	*Algernon C. Swinburne*	93
A BALLAD OF A BALLAD	*C. J. Stewart*	93
OLD FRENCH FORMS	*Clinton Scollard*	94
A RONDELET ON THE RONDELET	*Charles Henry Luders*	95
UN BON TRIOLET	*St-Amand*	96
A TRIOLET ON THE TRIOLET	*W. E. Henley*	96
ANOTHER	'*Stonyhurst Magazine*'	96
APOLOGY FOR THE TRIOLET	*I. P. Deane*	97
MY FIRST AND LAST TRIOLETS	*The Editor*	97
THE SONG	*T. H. Wright*	98
A QUATRAIN ON THE QUATRAIN	*Frank Dempster Sherman*	98
HEXAMETERS AND PENTAMETERS SELF-DESCRIBED	*Schiller, Coleridge, Longfellow*	98
OTHER METRES SELF-DESCRIBED	*The Editor*	100

SOME SONNET PRINCIPLES	101
POSTSCRIPT	115
INDEX OF AUTHORS	119

I.

THE STRUCTURE OF THE SONNET

> Et vous ne savez pas combien l'épreuve est rude
> De mener sans malheur le sonnet jusqu'au bout.
>
> *Sully Prudhomme*

Apollon de son feu leur fut toujours avare.
On dit, à ce propos, qu'un jour ce dieu bizarre,
Voulant pousser à bout tous les rimeurs françois,
Inventa du sonnet les rigoureuses loix ;
Voulut qu'en deux quatrains de mesure pareille
La rime avec deux sons frappât huit fois l'oreille,
Et qu'ensuite six vers artistement rangés
Fussent en deux tercets par le sens partagés.
Surtout de ce poème il bannit la licence,
Lui-même en mesura le nombre et la cadence,
Défendit qu'un vers faible y pût jamais entrer'
Ni qu'un mot déjà mis osât s'y remontrer.
Du reste il l'enrichit d'une beauté suprême.
Un sonnet sans défauts vaut seul un long poème.

     BOILEAU, *Art Poétique*, ii. 81-94.

The Earliest 'Soneto del Soneto'

Pedís, Reyna, un Soneto, y ya le hago;
   ya el primer verso y el segundo es hecho;
   si el tercero me sale de provecho,
con otro verso el un quarteto os pago.
Ya llego al quinto : España, Santiago !
   fuera, que entro en el sesto : sus, buen pecho :
   si del setimo salgo, gran derecho
tengo á salir con vida de este trago.

Ya tenemos á un cabo los quartetos :
   ¿ que me decís, Señora ? ¿ no ando bravo ?
mas sabe Dios si temo los tercetos.
   Y si con bien este Soneto acabo,
nunca en toda mi vida mas Sonetos,
   que de este, gloria á Dios, ya he visto el cabo.

        DIEGO HURTADO DE MENDOZA (1503–1575).

The same Translated

You ask a sonnet, lady, and behold !
   The first line and the second are complete.
   If equal luck I in the third should meet,
With one verse more the first quatrain is told.
St. James for Spain ! the fifth verse is outrolled—
   Now for the sixth.   'Twill be a gallant feat
   If after all I manage to retreat
Safe with my life from this encounter bold.

Already, rounded well, each quatrain stands.
   What say you, lady ?   Do I bravely speed ?
      Yet ah ! heaven knows the tercets me affright ;
And, if this sonnet were but off my hands,
   Another I should ne'er attempt indeed.
      But now, thank God, my sonnet's finished quite.

                              THE EDITOR.

The Second Spanish Sonnet on the Sonnet

Un soneto me manda hacer Violante :
   Y en mi vida me he visto en tal aprieto,
   Catorce versos dicen que es soneto,
Burla burlando van los tres delante.
Yo pensé que no hallara consonante,
   Y estoy á la mitad de otro cuarteto,
   Mas si me veo en el primer terceto
No hay cosa en los cuartetos que me espante.

Por el primer terceto voi labrando
   Y aun parece que entré con pié derecho,
Pues fin con este verso le voy dando.
   Ya estoy en el segundo, y aun sospecho,
   Que estoy los trece versos acabando :
   Contad si son catorce, y está hecho.

                    LOPE DE VEGA (1562–1635).

The same Translated

My haughty Fair a sonnet bids me make,
   I never was in such a fright before !
Why, fourteen lines, they say, those sonnets take :
   However, one by one, I have ek'd out four.
These rhymes, said I, I never shall complete,
   And found the second quatrain half way done!
If now the triplets had but all their feet,
   These first two quatrains pretty well might run.

On the first triplet thus I enter bold :
And, as it seems, my speed I still may hold ;
   Since the foundation is so fairly laid.
Now for the second. And so well dispos'd
My muse appears, that thirteen lines are clos'd.
Now count the whole fourteen ! The sonnet's made.

                    J. P. COLLIER.

Another Translation of the same

To write a sonnet doth Juana press me:
  I've never found me in such stress or pain;
  A sonnet numbers fourteen lines, 'tis plain.
And three are gone, ere I can say God bless me!
I thought that spinning rhymes might sore oppress me,
  Yet here I'm midway in the last quatrain;
  And if the foremost tercet I can gain,
The quatrains need not any more distress me.

To the first tercet I have got at last,
  And travel through it with such right good will,
    That with this line I've finished it, I ween;
I'm in the second now, and see how fast
  The thirteenth line runs tripping from my quill;
    Hurrah, 'tis done! Count if there be fourteen!
        JAMES YOUNG GIBSON.

The same Translated into French

Doris qui sait qu'aux vers quelquefois je me plais,
Me demande un sonnet, et je m'en désespère.
Quatorze vers, grand Dieu! le moyen de les faire?
En voilà cependant déjà quatre de faits.

Je ne pouvais d'abord trouver de rime, mais
En faisant on apprend à se tirer d'affaire.
Poursuivons, les quatrains ne m'étonneront guère
Si du premier tercet je puis faire les frais.

Je commence au hasard, et si je ne m'abuse,
Je n'ai pas commencé sans l'aveu de la muse,
Puisqu'en si peu de tems je m'en tire si net.

J'entame le second, et ma joie est extrême,
Car des vers commandés j'achève le treizième.
Comptez s'ils sont quatorze: et voilà le sonnet.
    ABBÉ RÉGNIER DESMARAIS (1632–1713).

An English Travesty

Capricious Wray a sonnet needs must have ;
  I ne'er was so put to 't before : a sonnet !
Why, fourteen verses must be spent upon it :
'Tis good, however, to have conquered the first stave.
Yet I shall ne'er find rhymes enough by half,
  Said I, and found myself i' the midst o' the second.
If twice four verses were but fairly reckon'd,
I should turn back on the hardest part, and laugh.

Thus far, with good success, I think I've scribbled
  And of the twice seven lines have got o'er ten.
Courage ! another 'll finish the first triplet ;
  Thanks to thee, Muse, my work begins to shorten :
There's thirteen lines got through, driblet by driblet ;
  'Tis done. Count how you will, I warrant there's fourteen.
          THOMAS EDWARDS (1699–1757).

On the Structure of the Sonnet

Apollo, at his crowded altars, tired
  Of votaries who, for trite ideas thrown
  Into loose verse, assume in lofty tone
The poet's name, untaught and uninspired,—
Indignant struck the lyre. Straight it acquired
  New powers and complicate. Then first was known
  The rigorous sonnet ; to be framed alone
By duteous bards, or by just taste admired.

'Go, energetic sonnet, go,' he cried,
  'And be the test of skill :—for rhymes that flow
Regardless of thy rules, their destined guide,
  Yet take thy name : ah, let the boasters know
That with strict sway my jealous laws preside,
  While I no wreaths on *rebel* verse bestow.'
          ANNA SEWARD (1747–1809).

The Agile Sonneteer

How facile 'tis to frame the sonnet! See:
   An 'apt alliteration' at the start;
   Phrase fanciful, turned t' other-end-to with art,
And then a rhyme makes 1st. and 4th. agree.

Ee words enough—so this next quatrain we
   Will therefore rhyme to match. Here sometimes 'heart'
   Comes in as 'hot' or 'throbbing,' to impart
A tang of sentiment to our idee.

Then the sextette, wherein there strictly ought
   To be a kind of winding up of things—
Only two rhymes, to have it nicely wrought,
   On which it settles, lark-like, as it sings:
   And so 'tis perfect, head and tail and wings.
'Lacks something?' Oh, as usual, but a thought.

Antony Morehead.

An American Sonnet on the Sonnet

Grant me twice seven splendid words, O Muse!
   (Like jewel pauses on a rosary chain
   To tell us where the *Aves* start again);
Of these, in each verse, one I mean to use—
Like Theseus in the labyrinth—for clues
   To help lost Fancy striving in the brain;
   And, Muse, if thou wilt still so kindly deign,
Make my rhymes move by courtly twos and twos!

Oh, pardon, shades of Avon and Vaucluse,
   This rush-light burning where your lamps yet shine;
A sonnet should be like the cygnet's cruise
   On polished waters; or like smooth old wine,
Or earliest honey garnered in May dews,
   And all be laid before some fair love's shrine.

Edith Thomas.

The Shaksperian Sonnet

If thou have only art mosaic-wise
   To cramp just fourteen lines in rhymes just five ;
If thou our Shakspere's sonnet half despise
   Because he strongly spurn'd so strict a gyve,
Because in fourteen lines seven rhymes he used,
   Because in that press'd couplet at the close
He loved to gather up his sweets diffused
   And pack them in the compass of a rose ;
If thou thus count upon thy fingers cold
   That music countable by souls alone,
Those sonnets with their cadences of gold,
   Little, yet living many an epic down—
Give thine own sonnets to the fire that lies
Fit grave for difficult stupidities.

ARCHBISHOP ALEXANDER.

The Petrarchan Sonnet

If thou canst mould thy work as Winter does,
   Who helps, not hides its beauty, line on line
   Intricately maintaining his design
Through all the fretwork and intaglios
Figured on frozen panes ; if to a rose
   A diamond thou canst cut ; it may be thine
   The sonnet's subtle secret to divine—
Chiefly if thou thy central thought dispose
So that through words by brevity made pale
   They who look wisely shall perceive at last
     The thought—as sometimes in a dim sea zone
   Through the grey mist there slowly grows a mast
Obscurely carrying noble heights of sail
   Miles through the dim magnificent unknown.

THE SAME.

SONNETEERING UNDER DIFFICULTIES

Well, if it must be so, it must; and I,
   Albeit unskilful in the tuneful art,
Will make a sonnet, or at least I'll try
   To make a sonnet and perform my part.
But in a sonnet everybody knows
   There must be always fourteen lines: my heart
Sinks at the thought! But courage! here it goes.
   There are seven lines already—could I get
Seven more, the task would be performed, and yet
It will be like a horse behind a cart,
For somehow rhyme has got a wondrous start
   Of reason, and, while puzzling on, I've let
The subject slip. What shall it be? But stay!
Here comes the fourteenth line. 'Tis done. Huzza!

          BISHOP FITZGERALD (1814–1883).

QUATRAINS AND TERCETS

I hear the quatrains' rolling melody,
   The second answering back her sister's sounds
   Like a repeated music, that resounds
A second time with varying harmony:

Then come the tercets with full-voiced reply,
   And close the solemn strain in sacred bounds,
   While all the time one growing thought expounds
One palpitating passion's ecstasy.

Ah! could I hear thy thoughts so answer mine
   As quatrain echoes quatrain, soft and low,
   Two hearts in rhyme and time one golden glow!
If so two lives one music might entwine,
What melody of life were mine and thine,
   Till song-like comes the ending all must know!

          GEORGE A. GREENE.

Le Sonnet
À Maître Claudius Popelin, émailleur et poète

Les Quatrains du sonnet sont de bons chevaliers
Crottés de lambrequins, plastronnés d'armoiries,
Marchant à pas égaux le long des galeries,
Ou veillant, lance au poing, droit contre les piliers.

Mais une dame attend au bas des escaliers ;
Sous son capuchon brun comme dans les féeries,
On voit confusément luire les pierreries,
Ils la vont recevoir, graves et reguliers.

Pages de satin blanc, à la housse bouffante,
Les Tercets, plus légers, la prennent à leur tour
Et jusqu'aux pieds du Roi conduisent cette Infante.

Là, relevant son voile, apparaît triomphante
La Bella, la Diva, digne qu'avec amour
Claudius, sur l'émail, en trace le contour.

    Théophile Gautier (1811–1872).

The same Translated
To Master Claudius Popelin, enameller and poet

Like most brave Cavaliers full richly dight
 In scalloped tunic, and surcoat with grace
 Of signs armorial, with measured movement pace
The Sonnet's Quatrains through the hall's long flight,
Or, lance in grip, watch by the pillar's height.
 Below, a maiden, whose brown hooded face
 Is gemm'd with mingling sheen of fairy trace,
Whom to receive they go with stately rite.

Like pages in white satin and puffed vest
 The lighter Tercets tend her in their turn
 And to the Royal Lover lead the maid :
There, in her joy triumphant, stands confessed
 The Queenly Beauty, one you would not spurn
 As worth her portrait by your hand inlaid.

    D. Moncrieff O'Connor.

A Second French Sonnet on the Sonnet

Pour le sonnet, huit ou dix pieds !
A douze, il prend des ampleurs lourdes ;
Le remplissage y met ses bourdes,
Vain bâton des estropiés.

Que de fléaux multipliés !
Les longueurs, les emphases sourdes,
Les adjectifs creux comme gourdes,
Chargent les vers humiliés.

Les douze pieds, c'est la charrette,
Pégase regimbe, il s'arrête,
Voyant qu'il faut prendre le pas.

Libre de cette peur fatale,
Sur huit pieds, fringant il détale,
Et, s'il crève, il ne traîne pas.
Louis Veuillot (1813–1883).

Un Autre

Un sonnet, dites-vous ; savez-vous bien, Madame,
    Qu'il me faudra trouver trois rimes à sonnet ?
Madame, heureusement, rime avec âme et flamme,
    Et le premier quatrain me semble assez complet.

J'entame le second, le second je l'entame,
    Et prends en l'entamant un air tout guilleret,
Car ne m'étant encor point servi du mot âme,
    Je compte m'en servir, et m'en sers en effet.

Vous m'accorderez bien, maintenant, j'imagine,
Qu'un sonnet sans amour ferait fort triste mine,
    Qu'il aurait l'air boiteux, contrefait, mal tourné.

Il nous faut de l'amour, il nous en faut quand même ;
J'écris donc en tremblant : Je vous aime, ou Je t'aime,
    Et voilà, pour le coup, mon sonnet terminé.
Henri Meilhac.

Das Sonett

Zwei Reime heiss' ich viermal kehren wieder,
  Und stelle sie, geteilt, in gleiche Reihen,
  Dass hier und dort zwei eingefasst von zweien
Im Doppelchore schweben auf und nieder.

Dann schlingt des Gleichlauts Kette durch zwei Glieder,
  Sich freier wechselnd, jegliches von dreien.
  In solcher Ordnung, solcher Zahl gedeihen
Die zartesten und stolzesten der Lieder.

Den werd' ich nie mit meinen Zeilen kränzen
  Dem eitle Spielerei mein Wesen dünket,
    Und Eigensinn die künstlichen Gesetze.

Doch, wem in mir geheimer Zauber winket,
Dem leih' ich Hoheit, Füll' in engen Grenzen,
  Und reines Ebenmass der Gegensätze.
        Augustus W. Schlegel (1767-1845).

The same Translated

Two rhyming sounds four times do I repeat,
  And these I so in even lines have placed,
  Two here, two there, by other two encased,
Their music floats in double cadence sweet.

Then winds the chain, more freely it is meet,
  Through two more measures, each three lines enlaced.
  The noblest and the tenderest strains have graced
This ordered metre and this rhythmic beat.

Ne'er will I crown him 'mid my favoured lovers
  Who deems my essence to be empty sounds
    And all these complex laws an idle whim.
But he my hidden magic who discovers,
  In these symmetric contrasts, these strait bounds,
    Power and riches I bestow on *him*.
        The Editor.

Another German Sonnet on the Sonnet

Du forderst ein Sonett von mir;
Du weisst, wie schwer ich dieses finde,
Darum, du lose Rosalinde,
Versprichst du einen Kuss dafür.

Was ist, um einen Kuss von dir,
Das sich Myrtill nicht unterstünde?
Ich glaube fast, ich überwinde;
Sieh, zwei Quatrains stehn ja schon hier!

Auf einmal hört es auf zu fliessen!
Nun werd' ich doch verzagen müssen!
Doch nein, hier ist schon Ein Terzett.

Nun beb' ich doch—Wie werd' ich schliessen?
Komm, Rosalinde, lass dich küssen!
Hier, Schönste, hast du dein Sonett.
Daniel Schiebeler.

A Third German Sonnet on the Sonnet

Dort, wo Musik und Sonne ist das Leben,
Bin ich ein süsses Spiel mit süssen Reimen;
Wie Lüftchen schmeicheln, Meereswellen schäumen,
Ist mir die Fülle goldnen Klangs gegeben.

Der Zauberschmuck kann nimmer mich umweben,
Vertief' ich mich in deutschen, stillen Räumen:
Hier in dem Wald lausch' ich der Geister Träumen,
Und das Gemüth lässt seine Saiten beben.

Dort bin ich Klang, der in die Luft zerfliesset;
Krystall hier, der Natur Hieroglyphe,
Ein Spiegel inn'rer Welt und inn'ger Triebe.

Der Vier und Drei und Sieben ernste Tiefe,
Den Bund, der sich durch Gegensätze schliesset,
Verkünd' ich so, in Sehnsucht und in Liebe.
Otto von Loeben.

An Italian Sonnet on the Sonnet

    Chi vuol saper ben tessere un sonetto
        Bastar non creda il musical concento
        Nè in quattordici righe aver ristretto
        Senza chiusa o premesse un argomento.
    Nuovo si elegga e non volgar soggetto
        Che degno sia di stabile ornamento ;
        E perchè suo vigor mostri il concetto,
        Si stia su verisimil fondamento.
    Se il verso ottavo e l'ultimo più terso
        Sostiene il polso e il sentimento esprime,
        Non sia 'l quinto all' undecimo.
    Vario il numero sia, dolce e sublime
        Abbia corpo la frase, anima il verso,
        Sian padroni i pensier, serve le rime.[1]

To a Scotch Tyro

Of fourteen lines your sonnet must consist,
    The first and fourth and fifth and eighth of which
    Will have their final syllables to hitch
In the same rhyme ; yet not with tortuous twist
Of words, but flowing kindly, e'en as kissed
    Melt into kisses baby-lips ; then rich
    In your authorities from Walker, pitch
The intervening lines, like harmonist
Most true, to one key-note. The closing six
In couplets or in triplets freely mix,
    Taking chief care, lest critics rate you on it,
The thought in its staid unity to fix.
    And then hurra ! fling high your tartan bonnet,
    For lo ! the thing is done—your maiden sonnet.
REV. J. J. JUDKIN.

---

[1] Sent by Christopher Ivanowich to Celio Fiorinelli.

What is a Sonnet?

What is a sonnet? 'Tis a form of poem
  Of fourteen lines, disposed in two quatrains
  With but two rhymes, of corresponding strains,
Alternate rhymed, or as here framed to show 'em:
And two tercets (or triplets, as we know 'em)
  Arranged at will; for here a choice obtains
  'Tween twice three ways; but (so its law ordains)
Into successive couplets ne'er to throw 'em.

The subject any; but, whate'er it be,
In one full thought, clear-claused, and blemish-free,
  With a beginning, middle, and an end.
    This, clearly, only given as a sample
Of its mere mechanism; both to blend,
  And illustrating precept by example.

                              M. MONTAGU.

Another Answer to the Same Question

What is a sonnet? 'Tis a silver bell
  That keepeth with its mates melodious chime;
  When swung by timid hand or lord of rhyme,
It rings faint music or to grand doth swell.
A flower of verse, it blooms in many a dell
  Of poesy; or, bird from Tuscan clime
  'Neath grayer skies, it sings in strains sublime
The mighty passions in the heart that dwell.

An opal, now it flashes sudden fire
  That smouldering in the soul to flame doth leap;
Or like a flute, whose note soars high and higher
  When touched by lips impassioned, doth it keep
The mind to heavens of thought, where broodings dire
  Are lotus-lulled into a dreamless sleep.

                              St. Mary's Chimes.

And Another

A sonnet is the body of a thought,
   Which enters suddenly the poet's mind
   And breathes its way, mysterious as the wind,
Unrecognised, as first it was unsought.
Whilst yet unformed, 'tis kindred to the Nought
   Whence it arose : the poet still must find
   Some spirit-worthy shape in which to bind
The subtle life wherewith his mind is fraught.

A stanza rises from the mental deep,
   Rhymes well disposed, with rhythm of even flow ;
     Full use of sense, due length of limb it gives,
A body fit. The thought, aroused from sleep,
   Flushes the rhythm with a poetic glow,
     And in the sonnet's form for ever lives.

ANON.

Rival Sonneteers

You said last night that you had tried a sonnet
   Which 'cross the street you'd send to let me see.
   Quite lost to guess what subject it may be,
I'm all anxiety that I should con it.
I hope no flea has got within your bonnet
   To make you think that you can rival me.
You'll rouse my ire, you may depend upon it :
   The very thought calls up my chivalry.

Don't mind, however, what above I've wrote ;
   Its beauties all my wrath may soon assuage,
   And, if 'tis good, adieu to all my rage !
And I'll transfer to you the fame I've got.
Of strictest rule I hope it bears the signs—
Right measured verse, and only fourteen lines.

JOHN ADAMSON.

The Sonnet Sonnetised

The sonnet is mechanical in part,
  In part ideal.   The cube root of song,
  Conceive in song, then build the verse along
In true Petrarchan style.   With rhythmic art
To all the fourteen lines a grace impart.
  Ten-syllable the verse, the rhymes be strong ;
  Within the octave only two belong,
And in the sestet three.   And here the heart
Of all the sonnet lies.   Concentred fast,
  Your thought, developed through each separate line,
    Here breaks the bounds and struggles to be free
Through hampering bars of rhyme ; and when the last
  Is reached, away it soars—a breath divine—
    In charmèd flight towards immortality.

Harriet H. Robinson.

Sonnet composed in the Concert Room at Northampton

'Could you compose a sonnet, amid all
This whirl of sound ?' a lady at my side
Inquired of me—to whom I nought replied ;
Tried to smile sagely, but no word let fall :
In sooth it seemed to me too capital
A difficulty to be so resolved
While lying yet on Sound's sea half dissolved,
Or tossed about by billows musical.
Yet had I often felt the soul of song
Pass into me, while yet the busy mind,
From its own subtle web scarce disentwined,
Lone paths obscure went wandering along ;
And harmony, unlooked for, undesigned,
Began to rule o'er thought's tumultuous throng.

Sir William Rowan Hamilton
(1805–1865).

Every Man his own Poet

You build a sonnet on about this plan :
   Your first line ground out, take the next one so :
   And make it rhyme with this one, just below.
Then, next you match the first line, if you can.
Don't hurry the machine. The lines must scan.
   With steady motion turn the crank. You know
   'Tis not a sonnet if it limps. Go slow.
Now find some rhyme for 'scan'—for instance, 'man.'

As to the last six lines, some latitude
   May be allowed. Take any word, as 'grove.'
Now hunt a rhyme for 'latitude.' Try 'shrewd.'
This line must end with 'dove,' or 'love,' or 'strove.'
And this with 'mood,' or 'prude,' or 'crude,' or 'dude' ;
   And there's your sonnet. Throw it in the stove.
                       The Chicago Tribune.

A Book of Sonnets

Thou who delight'st to view this goodly plot,
   Here take such flowers as best shall serve thy use,
Where thou may'st find in every curious knot,
   Of special virtue, and most precious juice,
Set by Apollo in their several places,
   And nourishèd with his celestial Beams,
And watered by the Muses and the Graces,
   With the fresh dew of those Castalian streams.
What scent or colour canst thou but devise
   That is not here, that may delight the sense ?
Or what can Art or Industry comprise,
   That in abundance is not gather'd hence ?
No garden yet was ever half so sweet
As where Apollo and the Muses meet.
          Belvedere ; or, The Garden of the Muses
                  (A.D. 1600).

Sonnet en Bouts-rimés

Veut-on savoir les loix du sonnet ? les voilà.
Il célèbre un héros, ou bien une Isabelle.
Deux quatrains, deux tercets, qu'on se repose là ;
Que le sujet soit un, que la rime soit belle.

Il faut dès le début qu'il attache déjà,
Et que jusqu'à la fin le génie étincelle,
Que tout y soit raison ; jadis on s'en passa ;
Mais Phébus la chérit ainsi que sa prunelle.

Partout dans un beau choix que la nature s'offre,
Que jamais un mot bas, tel que cuisine ou coffre,
N'avilisse le vers majestueux et plein,

Le lecteur chaste y veut une Muse pucelle
Enfin qu'aux derniers vers brille un éclat soudain,
Sans ce vain jeu de mots où le bon sens chancelle.
   HOUDART DE LA MOTTE (1672–1731).

Sonnet to a Rejected Sonnet

Poor child of Sorrow ! who didst boldly spring,
 Like sapient Pallas, from thy parent's brain,
 All armed in mail of proof! and thou wouldst fain
Leap further yet, and, on exulting wing,
Rise to the summit of the Printer's Press !
 But cruel hand hath nipp'd thy buds amain,
 Hath fix'd on thee the darkling inky stain,
Hath soil'd thy splendour, and defiled thy dress !
Where are thy 'full-orbed moon' and 'sky serene' ?
 And where thy 'waving foam,' and 'foaming wave' ?
All, all are blotted by the murd'rous pen,
 And lie unhonour'd in their papery grave !
Weep, gentle sonnets ! Sonneteers, deplore !
And vow—and keep the vow—you'll write no more !
   W. E. GLADSTONE (*Eton Miscellany*, 1827).

Don't!

Poet, beware ! The sonnet's primrose path
  Is all too tempting for thy feet to tread.
  Not on this journey shalt thou earn thy bread,
Because the sated reader roars in wrath :
' Little indeed to say the singer hath,
  And little sense in all that he hath said ;
  Such rhymes are lightly writ but hardly read,
And nought but stubble is his aftermath !'

Then shall he cast that bonny book of thine
  Where the extreme waste-paper basket gapes ;
There shall thy futile fancies peak and pine,
  With other minor poets, pallid shapes,
Who came a long way short of the divine,
  Tormented souls of imitative apes.
Daily News.

Woman and the Sonnet

Sonnet, be not rebellious in my hands
  That ply the spindle oftener than the lute !
  Without our woman's singing thou wert mute,
O sonnet, born of us in sunnier lands !

Think how the singing women trooped in bands
  To seek the greenwood, dancing to the flute.
  Hast thou forgot the refrain dissolute,
The circling dance, the chant, the ivied wands ?

Sonnet, a thousand years ago to-day
  Thou wast indeed the wild instinctive song
That women chanted for the Feast of May.

But now, O solemn mirror of the mind,
  Now it is I am weak, and thou art strong—
Keep me a coign of clearness, and be kind.
  A. M. F. ROBINSON (MADAME DARMESTETER).

II
THE NATURE OF THE SONNET

> Who read for me the sonnet, swelling loudly
> Up to its climax, and then dying proudly.
> *Keats*

Wordsworth was dimly conscious of this [his tendency to prolixity], and turned by a kind of instinct, I suspect, to the sonnet, because its form forced boundaries upon him and put him under bonds to hold his peace at the end of the fourteenth line. Yet even here nature would out, and the oft-recurring 'same subject continued' lures the nun from her cell to the convent parlour, and tempts the student to make a pulpit of his pensive citadel. The hour-glass is there, to be sure, with its lapsing admonition, but it reminds the preacher only that it can be turned.

JAMES RUSSELL LOWELL (1819-1891).

The Sonnet's scanty Plot of Ground.

Nuns fret not at their convent's narrow room;
And hermits are contented with their cells;
And students with their pensive citadels;
Maids at the wheel, the weaver at his loom,
Sit blithe and happy; bees that soar for bloom,
High as the highest peak of Furness-fells,
Will murmur by the hour in foxglove bells:
In truth, the prison unto which we doom
Ourselves, no prison is: and hence to me,
In sundry moods 'twas pastime to be bound
Within the sonnet's scanty plot of ground;
Pleased if some souls (for such there needs must be)
Who have felt the weight of too much liberty,
Should find brief solace there, as I have found.

WORDSWORTH (1770–1850).

On the peculiar Character of the Sonnet

Praised be the poet who the sonnet's claim,
  Severest of the orders that belong
  Distinct and separate to Delphic song,
Shall venerate, nor its appropriate name
Lawless assume. Peculiar is its frame,
  From him derived who shunned the city's throng
  And warbled sweet thy rocks and hills among,
Lonely Valclusa! And that heir of fame,
  Our greater Milton, hath by many a lay
Formed on that arduous model, fully shown
  That English verse may happily display
Those strict energic measures which alone
  Deserve the name of sonnet, and convey
A grandeur, grace, and spirit all their own.

ANNA SEWARD (1747–1809).

A Sonnet is a Sonnet

Ye whose aspirings court the Muse of lays,
  'Severest of those orders which belong
  Distinct and separate to Delphic song,'[1]
Why shun the sonnet's undulating maze ?
Or why its name, boast of Petrarchan days,
  Assume, its rules disowned ? Whom from the throng
The Muse selects, their ear the charm obeys
  Of its full harmony :—they fear to wrong
The sonnet by adorning with a name
  Of that distinguished import lays, though sweet,
  Yet not in magic texture taught to meet
Of that so varied and peculiar frame.
O think, to vindicate its genuine praise,
Those it beseems whose lyre a favouring impulse sways.

        CAPEL LOFFT (1751–1824).

Recantation

IN REPLY TO THE FOREGOING ADMONITION

Let the sublimer Muse, who, wrapt in night,
  Rides on the raven pennons of the storm,
  Or o'er the field, with purple havoc warm,
Lashes her steeds, and sings along the fight ;
Let her, whom more ferocious strains delight,
  Disdain the plaintive sonnet's little form,
  And scorn to its wild cadence to conform
The impetuous tenor of her hardy flight.
But me, far lowest of the sylvan train
  Who wake the wood-nymphs from the forest shade
  With wildest song ;—me, much behoves the aid
Of mingled melody, to grace my strain
And give it power to please, as soft it flows
Through the smooth murmurs of the frequent close.

        HENRY KIRKE WHITE (1785–1806).

[1] See the preceding sonnet. This one was addressed to Kirke White, who had published in the *Monthly Mirror* some 'quatorzains misnomered sonnets.'

Flowery Chains

If by dull rhymes our English must be chained,
   And, like Andromeda, the sonnet sweet
Fettered in spite of painèd loveliness ;
Let us find out, if we must be constrained,
   Sandals more interwoven and complete
To fit the naked feet of poesy ;
Let us inspect the lyre and weigh the stress
Of every chord, and see what may be gained
   By ear industrious and attention meet ;
Misers of sound and syllable, no less
Than Midas of his coinage, let us be
   Jealous of dead leaves in the bay-wreath crown,
So, if we may not let the muse be free,
   She will be bound with garlands of her own.
                JOHN KEATS (1795–1821).

A Moment's Monument

A sonnet is a moment's monument,
   Memorial from the soul's eternity
   To one dead deathless hour.   Look that it be,
Whether for lustral rite or dire portent,
Of its own arduous fulness reverent :
   Carve it in ivory or in ebony,
   As day or night may rule, and let Time see
Its flowering crest impearled and orient.

A sonnet is a coin : its face reveals
   The soul—its converse to what power 'tis due :
Whether for tribute to the august appeals
   Of Life, or dower in Love's high retinue,
It serve, or 'mid the dark wharf's cavernous breath
In Charon's palm it pays the toll to death.
          DANTE GABRIEL ROSSETTI (1828–1882).

Oh, for a Perfect Sonnet

Oh, for a perfect sonnet of all time !
  Wild music, heralding immortal hopes,
Strikes the bold prelude. To it from each clime,
  Like tropic birds on some green island slopes,
    Thoughts answering come, high metaphors, brave
      tropes,
In ordered measure, and majestic rhyme ;
  And presently all hearts, of kings and popes
And peoples, throb to this new theme sublime.

Anon 'tis reason speaks. A note of death
  Strengthens the symphony yet fraught with pain,
And men seek meanings with abated breath,
  Vexing their souls,—till lo, once more the strain
Breaks through triumphant, and Love's master voice
Thrills the last phrase and bids all joy rejoice.
                        WILFRID BLUNT.

The Sonnet's Voice

Yon silvery billows breaking on the beach
  Fall back in foam beneath the star-shine clear,
  The while my rhymes are murmuring in your ear
A restless lore like that the billows teach ;
For on these sonnet-waves my soul would reach
  From its own depths, and rest within you, dear,
  As through the billowy voices yearning here
Great nature strives to find a human speech.
A sonnet is a wave of melody ;
  From heaving waters of the impassioned soul
  A billow of tidal music one and whole
Flows in the ' octave' ; then returning free,
Its ebbing surges in the ' sestet' roll
  Back to the deeps of Life's tumultuous sea.
                        THEODORE WATTS-DUNTON.

On Reading the Preceding Sonnet

An art grows up from year to year : [1]
The critic weighs the utmost gains,
The last result, the perfect sphere,
Not the steps, but what remains ;

Sees the analogue, ebb and flow,—
Beautiful, yes, look at it near,—
The flow, the ebb returning so,—
It is at last art's perfect sphere.

But not the less our Shakespeare knew
Another way ; by full discourse
To show his picture as it grew,
Worked out in many-sided force ;

 Then when the heart can wish no more,
 With a strong couplet bars the door.
     WILLIAM BELL-SCOTT.

The Sonnet's Two Voices

Two voices are there : one is of the deep ;
 It learns the storm-cloud's thunderous melody,
 Now roars, now murmurs, with the changing sea,
Now bird-like pipes, now closes soft in sleep :
And one is of an old half-witted sheep
 Which bleats articulate monotony,
 And indicates that two and one are three,
That grass is green, lakes damp, and mountains steep.

And, Wordsworth, both are thine : at certain times
Forth from the heart of thy melodious rhymes
 The form and pressure of high thoughts will burst ;
At other times—good Lord ! I'd rather be
Quite unacquainted with the A. B. C.
 Than write such hopeless rubbish as thy worst.
    JAMES KENNETH STEPHEN (1859-1892).

---

[1] This smaller number of feet in each line is not allowed in English sonnets, but it is legitimate in French. See one of Louis Veuillot's, given on page 11, and a German sonnet, page 13.

What is the Sonnet?

What is the sonnet? 'Tis a flower whose seed
   Is some sublime emotion of the soul,
   That springeth into form as beautiful
As lily or violet, or winsome weed,
Or glowing rose, or daisy of the mead;
   Obedient to a lyrical control,
   Bursts into bloom, the theme of joy or dole,
Of hope or memory, noble thought or deed.
The wider realms of man's creative power
   Lie open to the mighty kings of song,
   To whom all things in heaven and earth belong;
But the kind Muse hath many a secret bower
   For humbler votaries—the gentle throng
Who cultivate the sonnet's fragrant flower.

                        HERBERT NEW.

Sonnet-Writing

Young men should not write sonnets, if they dream
Some day to reach the bright bare seats of fame:
To such, sweet thoughts and mighty feelings seem
As though, like foreign things, they rarely came.
Eager as men, when haply they have heard
Of some new songster, some gay-feathered bird,
That hath o'er blue seas strayed in hope to find
In our thin foliage here a summer home,
Fain would they catch the bright things in their mind,
And cage them into sonnets as they come.
No, they should serve their wants most sparingly
Till the ripe time of song, when the young thoughts
    fail;
Then their sad sonnets, like old bards, might be
Merry as youth, and yet grey-haired and hale.

            FATHER F. W. FABER (1814–1863).

On Receiving Main's 'Treasury of Sonnets'

Thou pretty sonnet that with measured pace
   Wouldst make my fancies walk, no more set free
   To roam the wildwood in their careless glee,
But chained by thee within a little space—
Thou mind'st me of some lovely girlish face
   From Reynolds' canvas, whose sweet roguery
   But borrows from her prim formality
Of pose and costume stiff a quainter grace.

Come, then, fair creature, with fit offering
   For him who bade me love thee for thyself,
     And courage taught to bind me with thy chain.
Yet since my voice is weak thy song to sing,
   Come, sweet tormentor! come, my tricksy elf,
     Come bring thy fairer sister whom he'll not disdain.

                    LILLAH CHABOT PERRY.

Three Sonnets on the Sonnet

I

The sonnet is a fruit which long hath slept
   And ripened on life's sun-warmed orchard-wall;
   A gem which, hardened in the mystical
Mine of man's heart, to quenchless flame hath leapt;
A medal of pure gold art's nympholept
   Stamps with love's lips and brows imperial;
   A branch from memory's briar, whereon the fall
Of thought-eternalising tears hath wept.

A star that shoots athwart star-steadfast heaven;
   A fluttering aigrette of tossed passion's brine;
   A leaf from youth's immortal missal torn;
A bark across dark seas of anguish driven;
   A feather dropped from breast-wings aquiline;
   A silvery dream shunning red lips of morn.

II

There is no mood, no heart-throb fugitive,
   No spark from man's imperishable mind,
   No movement of man's will, that may not find
Form in the sonnet and thenceforward live
A potent elf, by art's imperative
   Magic to crystal spheres of song confined ;—
   As in the moonstone's orb pent spirits wind
'Mid dungeon-depths day-beams they take and give.

Spare thou no pains ; carve thought's pure diamond
   With fourteen facets scattering fire and light.
   Uncut, what jewel burns but darkly bright ?
And Prospero vainly waves his runic wand
   If, spurning art's inexorable law,
   In Ariel's prison-sphere he leaves one flaw.

III

The sonnet is a world where feelings caught
   In webs of phantasy combine and fuse
   Their kindred elements 'neath mystic dews
Shed from the ether round man's dwelling wrought ;
Distilling heart's content, star-fragrance fraught
   With influences from the breathing fires
   Of heaven in everlasting endless gyres
Enfolding and encircling orbs of thought.

Our sonnet's world hath two fixed hemispheres :
   This, where the sun with fierce strength masculine
   Pours his keen rays and bids the noonday shine—
That, where the moon and stars, concordant powers,
   Shed milder rays and daylight disappears
   In low melodious music of still hours.

              JOHN ADDINGTON SYMONDS
                  (1840–1893).

Three more Sonnets on the Sonnet

I. THE LANE

Sunlit and broad the king's highway of song
   Lies yonder—but I tread it not, more fain
   To linger dreaming in this pleasant lane
Where oft, when weary seemed yon road and long,
Fame's pilgrims rested. Oh, what memories throng
   This little, narrow space! What love, what pain,
   These hedges know of! What high hopes, what vain
Desires, have here found utterance sweet or strong!

Here Shakspere hung his verse Orlando-wise
   On many a branch; here Dante sang of love;
   Sad Milton here forgot the evil days;
And still 't is echoing with Laura's praise—
   This lane, so straight, so small?—But, ah! above
What depth and vastness of the boundless skies!

II. THE VASE

Delicate, faultless, graceful as a dream
   Of Benvenuto—take and make it thine,
   This vase, young sculptor!—round the verge entwine
Myrtle and rue and bay; and fruitful theme
For thy deft chisel be yon forms that teem
   Through the Ivory Gate. Above them for a sign
   Alecton's whip and the shears of Proserpine,
And round the base carve Lethe's shadow'd stream.

Here fashion Eros, here the goat-foot Pan
   In a vale Arcadian; here the aegised might
     Of Pallas, and Urania's starry front;
     Here holy Vesta and the midnight hunt
   Of maiden Artemis; here the Lord of light,
And Heracles the champion of man.

III. THE WAYSIDE SHRINE

Fairer, Madonna, is thy face to me
In this straitened, rustic shrine beside the way,
Where skin-clad shepherds come to pipe and pray,
Where skies arch o'er us and the winds blow free,
And far-off gleams a luminous line of sea,
Than in the vast, thronged minster : there one may
To other loves and worships lightly stray,
But here the soul sees none, loves none but thee.

So to Guittone, too, as once along
This Tuscan way he rode and with bowed crest
And lowered lance made reverence, did it seem ;
Wherefore he built this little shrine of song
To hold one fair-wrought form—some memory blest,
Some hope, some happier thought, some idle dream.

INIGO PATRICK DEANE (1860–1894).

THE SONNETEER LIMITED

The lazy poet is the sonneteer,
  Who in twice-seven lines puts all he knows
  Of something, be it wood, or mead, or rose,
Or love, or hate—a wedding or a bier.
  He has his pattern always to his eyes ;
His thought can soar but in this narrow space,
And be it Niagara or a pretty face,
  The limit his expansion ever ties.
The rivulet, within its confined bed
  Of rock or clay, can seldom burst its banks ;
  Its song, though flushed, can never leave the ranks
Of small endeavours. With its proudest head
  'Tis but a small thing to the epic roar
  Old ocean dashes o'er a mighty shore.

EDWARD S. CREAMER.

Origin of the Sonnet

Soft sounding sonnet! Thee the Muse bestow'd
  On the short moments of some slave's repose;
  To the returning murmur of whose woes
Thy still returning rhyme congenial flow'd :
Ne'er through his measur'd hour the varying Ode
  Or stately Epic's lowering form arose;
  Toil taught his thoughts thy regulated close,
As the swift sand-glass bade resume his load.

Thy form succinct with sigh-resembling sound
  Of broken numbers did the winged Boy
Of Venus learn delighted : for he found
  Of short complaint, and, ah, far shorter joy,
Thee so expressive that he gently bound
    The vanquished Petrarch to thy fond employ.

                      THOMAS NOBLE.

Sonnet in Memory of a Sonnet-Writer[1]

I would that in the verse she loved, some word,
  Not all unfit, I to her praise might frame :
  Some word wherein the memory of her name
Should through long years its incense still afford.
But no, her spirit smote with its own sword;
  Herself has lit the fire whose blood-red flame
  Shall not be quenched : this is her loving fame
Who struck so well the sonnet's subtle chord.

None who e'er knew her can believe her dead;
  Though, should she die, they deem it well might be
Her spirit took its everlasting flight
  In summer's glory by the sunset sea—
That onward through the Golden Gate it fled.
  Ah, where that bright soul is cannot be night.

                      RICHARD WATSON GILDER.

[1] Mrs. Helen Hunt Jackson, author of 'Ramona,' well known in America by her maiden initials, 'H. H.' She died in California.

To a Critic

'It is but cunning artifice,' you say ;
  'To it no throb of nature answereth ;
  It hath no living pulse, no vital breath,
This puppet, fashioned in an elder day,
Through whose strait lips no heart can cry or pray.'
  O deaf and blind of soul, these words that saith !
  If that thine ear is dull, what hindereth
That quicker ears should hear the bugles play
And the trump call to battle ? Since the stars
  First sang together, and the exulting skies
    Thrilled to their music, earth hath never heard,
Above the tumult of her worldly jars,
  Or loftier songs or prayers than those that rise
    Where the high sonnet soareth like a bird.
Mrs. Julia Dorr.

To a Poet

Thou who wouldst wake the sonnet's silver lyre,
  Make thine hands clean ! Then, as on eagle's wings,
  Above the soiling touch of sordid things,
Bid thy soul soar till, mounting high and higher,
It feels the glow of pure celestial fire,
  Bathes in clear light, and hears the song that rings
  Through heaven's high arches when some angel brings
Gifts to the Throne, on wings that never tire !
It hath a subtile music, strangely sweet,
  Yet all unmeet for dance or roundelay,
    Or idle love that fadeth like a flower.
It is the voice of hearts that strongly beat,
  The cry of souls that grandly love and pray,
    The trumpet-peal that thrills the battle-hour !
Mrs. Julia Dorr.

A Dialogue on the Sonnet

A. What is a sonnet ?   Critic, tell me, pray !
B.   It is an epic in short space compressed ;
     The very life-blood of a poet's breast
Poured undiluted and spontaneously.
A. But has it rules which poets must obey ?
     How, then, spontaneous, if by chains oppressed
     The writer be ?   Why, 'twill be forced at best !
The bard like fettered prisoner at play.

B. The rules must be (as garb which one for long
     Has worn) familiar to the poet grown,
     Each rule, the most minute, not only known
          But felt : thus when the poet's glowing heart
          Has some great thought, with art concealing art
It springs spontaneous in the sonnet's song.

THOMAS AULD.

Sonnet Pauses

To write a sonnet on this empty page,
   Such is the task which I myself have set ;
   I swear I could perform, with less of fret,
In summer, fourteen miles of pilgrimage,
Nor seek a rest upon the four-mile stage
   (Which rest in sonnet journeying I get)
   But keep right on, with perspiration wet,
Till at the inn my room I should engage.

A summer's journey, fourteen miles in length,
   Were it divided as the sonnet is,
      How long the rest on the eighth mile would be !
Another pause—why, 'twould not try the strength
   Of one whom the great sun doth seldom kiss ;
      Since here the end of the last mile I see.

THOMAS AULD.

A Sonnet Simile

Oft have I seen upon the parchèd ground
   From summer clouds descend the cooling rain;
   Big drops all falling softly, till the plain
Grew black with moisture, by the sun embrowned
A moment past. Then the great sun uncrowned
   His head of clouds, and, shining forth again,
   From the hot land the vapours raised amain,
Till of the recent shower no trace was found.

Yet now more greenly shone the emerald leaf,
   The dust was laid, and cooled the sultry air.
And Fancy finds within the sonnet brief
     The falling rain, the vapour well defined,
     In 'octave,' and in 'sestet'; whilst the mind
Of him who reads receives refreshment rare.

THOMAS AULD.

The Sonnet's Golden Casket

As when a man invests with loving care
Some reliquary Time has sanctified,
Wherein his sainted gifts are set aside—
Each fond memorial of the days that were:
Sweet cherished secrets that were his to share,
Ere the full fervour of their passion died;
Time-tainted tokens of a joy denied,
Sworn vows yet unfulfilled—all homeing there!
So even I! Throughout the passing years
I gather up Life's best—its hopes and fears,
Its very sting, if but the soul should ask it;
For, ever faithful to my soul's command,
I take the little key with reverent hand,
And lock them in the sonnet's golden casket.

FERDINAND E. KAPPEY.

The Sacredness of the Sonnet

Why should the sonnet sound alone beside
The liquid music of Italian rill,
Or masquer's song, when all beside is still,
Where midnight serenaders softly glide,
Or in romantic groves at eventide,
To lute soft trembling at the lover's thrill?
For beauty is more beautiful, and song
More sweet when turned to high and sacred things;
Passion more pure, and all the lucid springs
Of music flow more lovelily along;
The movements of the heart more deep and strong;
And Fancy soars on brighter, better wings,
No tint, no splendour lost—but all is more
Enchanting and delightful than before.

JAMES EDMESTON.

A Caution to Sonneteers

A youthful poet found a form of verse,
As finds a child its faculty of throat,
And well he loved and tried his new-found note
Majestic, musical, and subtly terse.
And, like the child, the Bard reached higher strains,
As exercise and pattern gave him power,
Till, in the usance of his bounteous dower,
He freed himself from imperfection's pains.

There comes a waking time to child and man,
When what seemed best doth show itself to be
The very canker of complaisancie—
The infant's puppet fondled free from bran.
    As droops the butterfly beneath the touch,
    So fades the sonnet handled overmuch.

ELLIOT STOCK.

The Sonnet's Dignity

They err who say the sonnet is a toy
    For lazy bards to sport with in their leisure;
    Who weave one as an intellectual pleasure,
A careless metric pastime to enjoy.
And they degrade it, too, whose themes destroy
    The sacred purpose of this hallowed measure,
    Who use this precious casket for a treasure
Whose nature has some different alloy.

The passions are the only proper themes
    For this most tender, consecrated song,
        Which greatest singers have not done without.
It is the treasure-house of poet's dreams;
    And they who seek the door and listen long
        May hear the heart-throbs beat their passion out.

                        Allen Upward.

Terza Rima and the Sonnet

O *terza rima*, puzzle to the poet!
    By Dante much beloved but not by me—
    The bard from all such fetters should be free;
Freedom is sweet, and I shall ne'er forego it.
The sonnet, too, is quite vexatious, twining
With some small sense oft much Petrarchan whining.
Strange that a poet e'er should think of shining,
    Condemned to coop his thoughts in fourteen lines!
    Oft, when to write a sonnet she designs,
My wanton muse exceeds that scanty measure—
That is, when she's entirely at her leisure
And gives her wing free scope with purest pleasure:
    High over earth she spreads her flight afar,
    Chainless as winds that sweep the mountain are.

                        James Haskin.

A Hidden Acrostic

'Seldom we find,' says Solomon Don Dunce,
    'Half an idea in the profoundest sonnet.
Through all the flimsy things we see at once
    As easily as through a Naples bonnet—
    Trash of all trash! How can a lady don it?—
Yet heavier far than your Petrarchan stuff,
Owl-downy nonsense that the faintest puff
    Twirls into trunk-paper the while you con it.'
And, veritably, Sol is right enough.
The general tuckermanities are arrant
Bubbles—ephemeral and so transparent.
    But this is, now,—you may depend upon it—
Stable, opaque, immortal—all by dint
Of the dear names that lie concealed within 't.[1]

        EDGAR ALLAN POE (1809–1849).

Multum in Parvo

The sonnet is the cherished Rose de Meaux
Of poesy all perfect in its kind
Albeit small. It is a cameo,
Of size just fitted on the heart to bind.
The poet and initiated know,
And they alone, the beauties of this gem
The choicest in the Muse's diadem,
Whose classic form we to Italia owe.

It is an oratory off the aisle
Of the cathedral epic, interlaced
With ornaments elaborate yet chaste
And not unworthy of the grander pile.
It is a dome whose just proportion veils
Its amplitude, and seemingly curtails.

        JAMES COCHRANE.

[1] The first letter of first line, second of second, etc., put in order, form 'Sarah Anna Lewis.' 'Tuckermanities,' from an American verse-writer, Henry T. Tuckerman (1813–1870).

Communia Proprie

The earth is common : witness how its name
Falls through thy watchful mind and not a care
Disturbs the fancy whence or why it came :
To all the careless world 'tis dead and bare.
But cast it out a million miles in air,
Breathe on it silver light or golden flame,
Give it life, movement, radiance, soft and fair,
And all the world will wonder at its fame.

This is the sonnet ; cast about men's doors,
The tool in common hands is cheap and poor ;
But born from out a soul that gently soars
In sweeter air, though on some sunless moor,
It still must live, warm in its mother's fire :
Eros sublime, still bending o'er his lyre.

ANON.

From the Great Deep

Art gave it us as Nature doth a shell :
    It holds the murmurings of the infinite deep
        Of mind and thought ; through its small arches creep
The voices born about the sacred well ;
Shakespeare hath breathed into it, and here dwell
    Those trumpet-tones that never die or sleep.
    Listen ! the souls of poets it doth keep
Shut in its chambers by some potent spell.
Whate'er the seas have whispered to the lands
    A shell repeats ; this sings the heart's own lay.
But when I raised it dripping from the sands
    To bear it to my cabinet, woe the day !
The tiny treasure brake within my hands,
    And all its music fled from it away.

S. V. COLE.

Two Sonnets on the Sonnet

I

To different men the same thing different seems,
   According to the place where they may be,
   Or to the light in which they chance to see—
The day's clear glow, or evening's glimmering gleams.
The mind of man, kaleidoscopic, teems
   With many a fanciful, rich simile,
   Consistent with its mood. Soft reverie
Brings other pictures than those brought by dreams.
One,[1] on the marge of thought's mysterious main,
   A shell, whose echoing chambers ne'er are mute,
   Finds in the sonnet, marvelling in the sound;
Another,[2] a small pipe of cheery strain,
   A myrtle leaf, a key, a lamp, a lute,
   A trumpet, or a scanty plot of ground.

II

'Within the sonnet's scanty plot of ground,'
   By Fancy led, I lazily rove at ease—
   A vale luxuriant, girt with shadowy trees,
And lulled by a small rivulet's tinkling sound;
Where nod and smile fair wild-flowers all around,
   Charmed by the bagpipes of the belted bees,
   Whose drone, and songs of birds, and murmur of breeze,
Together in links of harmony are bound.
There, through a glimmering outlook, I behold,
   Gleaming afar, the purple peak of Fame,
Crowned with its temple; to mine ear is rolled
The city's hum, mixed with the low of herds,
   While, musing, I, an idler, carve my name
On a smooth beech, and give to the air my words.

W. L. SHOEMAKER.

---

[1] S. V. Cole in the preceding Sonnet.   [2] Wordsworth.

Das Sonett

Sich in erneutem Kunstgebrauch zu üben
  Ist heil'ge Pflicht, die wir dir auferlegen.
  Du kanst dich auch, wie wir, bestimmt bewegen
Nach Tritt und Schritt, wie es dir vorgeschrieben.

Denn eben die Beschränkung lässt sich lieben,
  Wenn sich die Geister gar gewaltig regen;
  Und wie sie sich denn auch geberden mögen,
Das Werk zuletzt ist doch vollendet blieben.

So möcht' ich selbst in künstlichen Sonetten
  In sprachgewandter Masse kühnem Stolze,
  Das Beste, was Gefühl mir gäbe, reimen;

Nur weiss ich hier mich nicht bequem zu betten;
  Ich schneide sonst so gern aus ganzem Holze
  Und müsste nun doch auch mitunter leimen.

GOETHE (1749–1832).

The same Translated

The sinews of the soul to energise
  For Art's new needs—this the high task we fain
  Would lay upon thee, for thou mov'st amain
Thy feet, though fettered, in most artful wise.

The fetter's self do we not learn to prize
  When spirits over-wild chafe round the brain?
  From their keen vigour, curbed by prudent chain,
The perfect work at length doth glad the eyes.

And I were 'mong the poets proud and blest,
Could I, too, tune my fancy's, feeling's, best
To a fair sonnet's verse unblameable.

But not for me such dainty mould! Too well
I've loved to rough-hew from the oak's broad breast,
Or roughly joint the fragments as they fell.

GEORGE O'NEILL, S.J.

"Même avec Cent Défauts"

Vous prenez, Lélio, ce certain air benêt
Qui fait que certains jours vous n'êtes plus le même :
Vous voilà circonspect, timide, tout en crème . . .
Que nous a, cette nuit, couvé votre bonnet ?

Ne faites pas le fin, poète ; on vous connaît !
Produisez ce chef-d'œuvre et quittez le ton blême.
Un sonnet, je parie ? . . Eh bien donc ! Un sonnet,
Même avec cent défauts, vaut mieux qu'un long poème.[1]

On aurait tort d'en pondre un millier par saison !
Mais le gout du sonnet, bridé par la raison,
Est innocent.   Bernez les railleurs, gent frivole !
De la rime abondante il corrige l'abus,
Il met dans un corset la pensée un peu molle,
Il aide à bien passer le temps en omnibus.

Louis Veuillot.

"Un Sonnet sans Défaut"

Un sonnet sans défaut vaut seul un long poème,
A dit certain gâteux du temps du roi-soleil.
Un bon sonnet, pour moi, c'est une joie extrême,
Un régal délicat, un bijou sans pareil.

J'ai pâli bien souvent, ami, sur ce problème :
Faire aussi mon sonnet !   A l'horizon vermeil
Un rêve me montrait une pensée, un thème,
Qui s'évanouissait souvent à mon réveil.

Quand, revenant à moi, je saisissais la plume,
Pour fixer ce croquis estompé dans la brume,
Hélas ! de mon esprit le vent l'avait banni.

Aussi, sans plus chercher, je me tais, j'y renonce,
Ce n'est pas un sonnet qui sera ma réponse.
Tiens !—mais, sans y songer, mon sonnet est fini.

Ernest Lacoste.

---

[1] Alluding to Boileau's famous lines which have been given at p. 2.

Sonnet contre le Sonnet

Au diable le sonnet, bien que dans la Sicile
Il ait longtemps fleuri dans les vallons d'Enna !
N'est pas toujours très beau ce qu'on croit difficile,
Et Boileau, sur ce point, sottement raisonna.

Quant à moi, je préfère un seul vers de Virgile
A ce vain jeu d'esprit qui nous vint de l'Etna,
Il peut plaire à la cour et sourire à la ville ;
Le bon sens indigné par tout le condamna.

Le plus beau ne vaut pas le moins brillant poème,
Car loin d'être enrichi d'une beauté suprême,
Auprès d'un diamant, c'est un caillou du Rhin.

Le verre imite mal le cristal de Bohême.
Le sonnet, c'est le verre, et la vierge que j'aime
Rejetterait le strass de son splendide écrin.

Th. Richard-Baudin.

Boileau again

Voulant te rogner l'aile, ô libre poésie !
Un sévère critique et peu lyrique auteur
Soutint que le sonnet est une œuvre choisie
Dont rien ne peut, en vers, atteindre la hauteur.

Maintenant, pour Boileau, pédant législateur,
Nous ne témoignons pas beaucoup de courtoisie :
Nous l'appelons perruque, et du vieux radoteur
Nous raillons volontiers la docte fantaisie.

Nos poètes du jour, il est vrai, sont plus forts.
Ils maîtrisent la langue et riment sans efforts.
Le métier ne voit plus l'ouvrage de la veille.

Quant à moi, pour finir le travail que voici,
Mon cerveau n'a pas eu grand' peine, Dieu merci !
Et j'avoue humblement n'avoir pas fait merveille.

Léon Magnier.

Le Sonnet

Dans sa forme attrayante, avec art modelée,
Nous aimons le sonnet, concis et gracieux.
Nous le voulons parfait : accents harmonieux,
    Œuvre finement ciselée.

Elevant son essor vers la voute étoilée,
Dont les astres sans nombre éblouissent nos yeux,
Ainsi que l'ode il peut, dans l'infini des cieux,
    Monter sur une stance ailée.

Souvent le cœur y parle un langage charmant ;
L'esprit en fait jaillir comme d'un diamant
    Les plus brillantes étincelles.

Oui, c'est un joyau rare, une perle, un trésor...
Avouons-le pourtant : c'est une cage d'or
    Où n'entrent pas les grandes ailes.

Léon Magnier.

Le Sonnet est Limousin

    L'Apologue est indien ;
    L'Attique trouva le Drame ;
    L'Elégie est de Pergame ;
    Le Poème est rhodien.

    Un berger arcadien
    Composa l'Epithalame ;
    L'inventeur de l'Epigramme
    Fut le barbier lydien.

    Enna fit parler Tityre ;
    Rome conçut la Satire ;
    Bysance orna le Dizain ;

    La Ballade est allemande ;
    La Villanelle, normande ;
    Et le Sonnet, limousin !

Abbé Joseph Roux.

A Tailor-made Jacket

Je n'entrerai par là—dit la folle en riant—
   Je vais faire éclater ce corset de Procruste.
   Puis, elle enfle son sein, tord sa hanche robuste,
Et prête à contre-sens un bras luxuriant.

J'aime ces doux combats, et je suis patient,
   Dans l'étroit vêtement qu'à sa taille j'ajuste,
   Là, serrant un atour, ici le déliant,
J'ai fait passer enfin tête, épaules, et buste.

Avec art maintenant dessinons sous ses plis
La forme bondissante et le contours polis ;
   Voyez ! la robe flotte, et la beauté s'accuse.

Est-elle bien ou mal en ces simples dehors ?
Rien de moins dans le cœur, rien de plus sur le corps,
   Ainsi me plaît la femme, ainsi je veux la Muse.

JOSÉPHIN SOULARY.

'Ut Pictura Poesis'

Dans l'Epopée, une vaste peinture
   S'enlève à fresque et se brosse à grands traits ;
   Des demi-dieux violant les secrets,
Le Drame antique outre un peu la nature ;

Jusqu'aux confins de la caricature
   La Comédie exhaussant ses portraits,
   Nous fait toucher nos travers de plus près ;
Le Sonnettiste est peintre en miniature :

De Michel-Ange il n'a pas les crayons,
De Raphaël les célestes rayons,
   Ou de Rubens la magique palette ;

Terburg, Miéris lui prêtent leur pinceau :
   L'immensité dans la mer se reflète ;
Un coin du ciel suffit au clair ruisseau.

GEORGES GARNIER.

The Sonnet-in-Law

Du sonnet quel est l'avantage ?
   Vous dit-on souvent au palais :
   Il n'a que faire dans les plaids,
Ce n'est qu'un charmant badinage.

Erreur ! on doit à son usage
   De condenser, non sans succès,
   En peu de mots, en quelques traits,
Un confus et lourd verbiage.

Eh quoi ! messieurs les avocats,
Quatorze vers sont-ils au cas
   D'encourir votre raillerie ?

Onques juge ne dormirait
   Si jamais une plaidoirie
N'était plus longue qu'un sonnet.
G. Hipp.

Pourquoi des Sonnets ?

Comme au bonhomme La Fontaine,
   'Les longs ouvrages me font peur ;'
A mon esprit de courte haleine
   Convient un facile labeur.

Pourtant je ne crains pas la peine,
   Et je ne suis pas sans ardeur ;
Mais de la source d'Hippocrène
   Par gouttes me vient la liqueur.

Non plus qu'à nos anciens trouvères,
Il ne me faut pas de grands verres
   Pour trinquer avec Apollon.

Du Sonnet la faible mesure
Suffit pour rendre mon allure
   Titubante au sacré vallon.
A. Boursault.

Le Sonnet et le Siècle

Dans cette époque ardente où la vapeur est reine,
Où les jours, plus pressés, pour tous semblent courir,
L'idéal, exilé de sa sphère sereine,
De rêves longs et doux ne peut plus se nourrir.

Le fait parle en despote et sa voix souveraine
Nous dit : il faut marcher et ne plus discourir,
Car la vie aujourd'hui n'est qu'une grande arène,
Où l'on entre à son tour pour lutter et mourir.

Dans cette course folle, où s'agiter c'est vivre,
Eh ! qui donc a le temps de composer un livre,
Comme pour le présent écrit pour l'avenir ?

Le sonnet, dans sa forme exacte et condensée,
Répond à notre hâte, en servant la pensée,
Et par un dernier trait l'impose au souvenir.

Auguste de Vaucelle.

Sonnettistes, à l'œuvre !

Dans les trompes d'argent, ô fanfares, sonnez !
Qu'à vos bruyants appels ne résiste personne,
Car les épis sont mûrs et la moisson foisonne ;
Sonnettistes, à l'œuvre ! Allez et moissonnez !

Prenez tous votre essor, ô chantres des sonnets,
En rhythme éolien que le luth d'or résonne !
L'essaim ailé des vers autour de vous frissonne,
Dans deux quatrains égaux l'un à l'autre enchaînés.

Au cliquetis joyeux de leur double cadence,
Secouant les grelots de la rime qui danse,
Les tercets accouplés chantent à l'unisson.

Sonnettistes, laissez envoler vos pensées,
Avec des nœuds de fleurs l'une à l'autre enlacées,
Et mariez toujours l'idée avec le son !

J. B. Gaut.

Al Sonetto

Quand' io ti sveglio e al corpo il lin più raro
    Ti vesto e i fiori sul capo ti metto,
    Ed in quell' opra sì pieno è il diletto
Che non ci sento mai stilla d' amaro,

E come padre per tenero affetto
    Con te converso, figliolin mio caro,
    Non so perchè gli arcavoli sognaro
Paragonarti di Procruste al letto.

Naturalmente se non sei che un grullo
    O tisicuzzo sin da la matrice,
    E tormento vestirti e non trastullo.

Ma se fra l' erbe scherzi ilare e sano,
    Gli arcavoli hanno torto, e noi si dice
    Che il letto di Procruste è un sogno vano.

                            G. Prati.

The Sonnet of a Septuagenarian

A plaintive sonnet flowed from Milton's pen
    When Time had stolen his three-and-twentieth year:
    Say, shall not I, then, shed one tuneful tear,
Robbed by the thief of three-score years and ten?
No! for the foes of all life-lengthened men,
    Trouble and toil, approach not yet too near;
    Reason, meanwhile, and health, and memory dear
Hold unimpaired their weak yet wonted reign:
Still round my sheltered lawn I pleased can stray;
    Still trace my sylvan blessings to their spring:
Being of Beings! yes, that silent lay
    Which musing Gratitude delights to sing,
Still to thy sapphire throne shall Faith convey,
    And Hope, the cherub of unwearied wing.

                    William Mason (1724–1797).

Sonnet-Gold

I

We get it from Etruscan tombs, hid deep
    Beneath the passing ploughshare ; or from caves,
    Known but to Prospero, where pale green waves
Roll up the wreck-gold that the mermaids keep ;
And from the caverns where the gnomes upheap
    The secret treasures which the Earth's dwarf slaves
Coin in her bosom, till the red gold paves
Her whole great heart, where only poets peep ;

Or from old missals, where the gold defies
    Time's tooth, in saints' bright aureoles, and keeps,
In angels' long straight trumpets, all its flash ;
But mostly from the crucible where lies
    The alchemist's pure dream-gold : while he sleeps,
The poet steals it, leaving him the ash.

II

What shall we make of sonnet-gold for men ?
    The dove-wreathed cup some youth to Phryne gave ?
    Or dark Locusta's scent-phial, that shall have
Chiselled all round it snakes from Horror's den ?
Or that ill ring which sank in fathoms ten
    When Faliero spoused the Venice wave ?
    Or Inez' funeral crown, the day the grave
Showed her for coronation, all myrrh then ?

The best would be to make a hilt of gold
    For Life's keen falchion ; like a dragon's head
Fierce and fantastic, massive in your hold ;
But oft the goldsmith's chisel makes instead
    A fretted shrine for sorrows that are old,
And passions that are sterile or are dead.

                        Eugene Lee-Hamilton.

III.

THE MASTERS OF THE SONNET

> Fretting with skilless touch the sonnet's wire :
> Alas, the strings of this small harp require
> To bring forth half their worth a master's hand.
>
> *Ebenezer Elliot*

The graver by Apollo's shrine,
Before the gods had fled, would stand,
A shell or onyx in his hand,
To copy there the face divine,
Till earnest touches, line by line,
Had wrought the wonder of the land
Within a beryl's golden band,
Or on some fiery opal fine.

Ah! would that as some ancient ring
To us, on shell or stone, doth bring
Art's marvels perished long ago,
So I, within the sonnet's space,
The large Hellenic lines might trace,
The statue in the cameo.

ANDREW LANG.

Scorn not the Sonnet

Scorn not the sonnet; Critic, you have frowned
Mindless of its just honours. With this key
Shakespeare unlocked his heart; the melody
Of this small lute gave ease to Petrarch's wound;
A thousand times this pipe did Tasso sound;
With it Camoens soothed an exile's grief;
The sonnet glittered a gay myrtle leaf
Amid the cypress with which Dante crowned
His visionary brow; a glow-worm lamp,
It cheered mild Spenser, called from Faery-land
To struggle through dark ways; and when a damp
Fell round the path of Milton, in his hand
The Thing became a trumpet; whence he blew
Soul-animating strains—alas, too few!
WORDSWORTH.

The same imitated in French

Ne ris point des sonnets, ô critique moqueur;
Par amour autrefois en fit le grand Shakespeare;
C'est sur ce luth heureux que Pétrarque soupire,
Et que le Tasse aux fers soulage un peu son cœur;

Camoens de son exil abrége la longueur,
Car il chante en sonnets l'amour et son empire;
Dante aime cette fleur de myrte, et la respire,
Et la mêle au cyprès que ceint son front vainqueur.

Spenser, s'en revenant de l'île des féeries,
Exhale en longs sonnets ses tristesses chéries;
Milton, chantant les siens, ranimait son regard:

Moi! je veux rajeunir le doux sonnet en France,
Du Bellay, le premier, l'apporta de Florence,
Et l'on en sait plus d'un de notre vieux Ronsard.
SAINTE-BEUVE (1804–1869).

The same parodied at New York

Scorn not the meerschaum.   Housewives, you have croaked
  In ignorance of its charms.   Through this small reed
  Did Milton, now and then, consume the weed;
The poet Tennyson hath oft evoked
The Muse with glowing pipe, and Thackeray joked
  And wrote and sang in nicotinian mood;
  Hawthorne with this hath cheered his solitude;
A thousand times this pipe hath Lowell smoked;
Full oft have Aldrich, Stoddard, Taylor, Cranch,
  And many more whose verses float about,
    Puffed the Virginian or Havana leaf;
And when the poet's or the artist's branch
  Drops no sustaining fruit, how sweet to pout
    Consolatory whiffs—alas! too brief!

Harper's Magazine.

The same supplemented

And other poets, of no meaner name
  Than Sydney, the accomplished among men,
  And Jonson's valued friend of Hawthornden,
Have penned the sonnet.   He whose deathless fame
No humble verse like mine can fitly frame,
  Ill-fated Raleigh, in most happy vein
  One witching sonnet on the Faery Queen
Hath breathed, which sternest critics durst not blame.

Of moderns, who like Wordsworth can set forth
  This little gem in colours fair and bright,
  Of various hues, like the celestial light
Of differing stars that stud the Polar North?
In these, as set in amber things of worth,
  Live thoughts profound, shines many a fairy sprite.

ARCHDEACON BENJAMIN BAYLEY.

Scorn it if you will!

'Scorn not the sonnet!' Scorn it if you will,
   It shall outlive and conquer scorn and you,
Thrive like a hardy plant, and drink its fill
   Of rain and wind as of the sun and dew.
Not murmuring dreams and loves of Italy,
   Not bent in bars of artificial rule;
No, but the English sonnet, strong and free,
   The heart its master and the world its school:
For manly love and grave devotion meet,
   Meet for the happy voice of lighter hours,
But rendering, when the hearts of nations beat
   And we just hear the stir of sleeping powers,
A deep and solemn music to become
At need the stern roll of the menacing drum.
               FRANCIS HEYWOOD WARDEN.

Toy of the Titans!

Toy of the Titans! Tiny Harp! again
I quarrel with the order of thy strings,
Established by the law of sonnet-kings,
And used by giants that do nought in vain.
Was Petrarch, then, mistaken in the strain
That charms Italia? Were they tasteless things
That Milton wrought? And are they mutterings
Untuneful, that pay Wordsworth with pleased pain?
No. But I see that tyrants come of slaves,
That states are won by rush of robbers' steel,
And millions starved and tortured to their graves,
Because as they are taught men think and feel;
Therefore I change the sonnet's slavish notes
For cheaper music, suited to my thoughts.
               EBENEZER ELLIOT (1781–1849).

The Powers of the Sonnet

Why should the tiny harp be chained to themes
In fourteen lines with pedant rigour bound?
The sonnet's might is mightier than it seems:
Witness the bard of Eden lost and found,
Who gave this lute a clarion's battle-sound.
And lo! another Milton calmly turns
His eyes within on light that ever burns,
Waiting till Wordsworth's second peer be found.
Meantime Fitzadam's mournful music shows
That the scorn'd sonnet's charm may yet endear
Some long deep strain, or lay of well-told woes
Such as in Byron's couplet brings a tear
To manly cheeks, or o'er his stanza throws
Rapture and grief, solemnity and fear.

EBENEZER ELLIOT.

To Thomas Bailey Aldrich, on his Sonnets

Delightful troubadour, on whatso theme
  You choose to link your dainty thoughts together,
Within the 'sonnet's scanty plot' they gleam
  Like gay-winged birds confined with silken tether.
There, in your fancy's glow, to me they seem
  To sing like soaring larks in summer weather,
Or nightingales that thrill the rose's dream
  With moonlight song while love thrills every feather.
You, Camoens, by the Tagus' golden strand,
  You, in Hesperia, learned Boccaccio,
  And he who Laura lauded day and night,
Hafiz, Firdousi, and Saadi, in Samarcand
  Or Ispahan, had crowned with praise, I know;
  In Albion, Daniel;—such sweet rhymes you write.

II

Sonnets do not spring up like wild-wood flowers,
   O'er the green grass, and brown, dead leaves thick-strewed
In fair perfection, when the cold and rude
Snow-storms give place to Ver's reviving showers.
Artfully-framed, they tax a poet's powers,
   And are no product of a lucky mood,
   But slowly-wrought as nests are, where the brood
Bides long ere its full music thrills the bowers.
To accident and sudden inspiration
   They owe no more than do the lovely chimes
   Rung on accordant bells ; nor in a twinkling
Grows into birth their tuneful modulation :
   Labour, skill, patience, mastery over rhymes—
   From these proceed they, pranked and finely tinkling.

III

All these have you, ' enamoured architect
   Of airy rhyme,' accomplished sonneteer—
   You whom I sometimes think without a peer
In framing sonnets free from all defect,
So seeming artless one would not suspect
   Your art in hiding art, while you the ear
   Charm as with music of some heavenly sphere,
By the melodious words which you select.
Polished as Grecian epigrams are they ;
   Sparkling as gems the patient toil of man
   Makes fitting ornament for beauty's breast ;
Faultless as flowers that strew the path of May :
   No poet in the land Italian
   Thought in this garb more richly ever dressed.

W. L. Shoemaker.

The Treasure Bark

There sails a little bark on the wide sea
  Of letters, gay with golden bells of rhyme,
  Making, as on it speeds, melodious chime,
And with rare jewels laden copiously.
The helmsman most of love sings loud and free,
  Being love's liege ; but oft, in strains sublime,
  Of truth victorious, leagued with patient time ;
Of beauty, her kin ; of right and liberty.
Since Fra Guittone first this slender boat
  Italian trimmed, have poets of renown
  Trusted great treasure of rich thought upon it.
While sinks the ponderous epic, still afloat,
  A magic craft, it fears no tempest's frown ;
  The breath of fame, propitious, wafts the sonnet.

                    W. L. SHOEMAKER.

A Golden Climax

One thought expanding as it wings along
  In normal rhyme, and gathering while it goes
Fresh force and illustration, never long
  Delaying on a point, as one who knows
  His time is short, or as a flower that blows
At dawn, matures when noontide heat is strong,
  And perishes in evening's mellow close ;
The artful measure of a stately song.
Such is the sonnet, when through Petrarch's page
  Its plaintive course melodiously it wends,
Or—Sydney's, Milton's, Wordsworth's heritage—
  Immortal down the tide of letters sends
The lover's sigh, the sentence of the sage,
  And in a golden climax sweetly ends.

                    JOHN CHARLES EARLE.

Apology for Translating Petrarch

The dark-eyed stranger from yon sunny clime,
  An exile 'neath our colder, cloudier skies,
  For native brightness, native gladness sighs,
  And the soft speech that yields the softer rhyme;
Sighs for the Love he knew in happier time,
  In the responsive sunshine of her eyes;
  Sighs 'mid the coldness of the worldly-wise
Who dull their sense of beauty in their prime.
So these sweet sonnets in my rougher speech,
  As exiles, lose their native loveliness,
  The tones unheard of Dante's, Petrarch's lyre;
But should they lead thee upward till thou reach
  Their burning source, to greater from much less,
  I need not blush for my reflected fire.

Charles Tomlinson.

The Masters

O matchless verse, whether we look at thee
In honeyed parts, or as a perfect whole!
Simple yet subtle, speaking to the soul
As can no other form of poetry;
Soft, lithe and graceful, yet so strong we see,
That, when they would the heart entire control,
Its passions rouse or all its griefs condole,
The Masters chose thy pliant melody!

O then when Shakespeare took thee to his heart,
When Petrarch languished all thy power to sway,
What secret sweetnesses did they discover,
What loves immortal to the world impart!
And Milton, surely, hath left songs which say
That thou couldst aid the patriot, as the lover.

Francis P. McKeon.

What is a Sonnet?

Fourteen small, baleful berries on the hem
   Of Circe's mantle, all of greenest gold;
   Fourteen of lone Calypso's tears that roll'd
Into the sea, for pearls to come of them.
Fourteen small signs of omen in the gem
   With which Medea human fate foretold;
   Fourteen small drops, which Faustus, growing old,
Craved of the Fiend to water life's dry stem.

It is the pure white diamond Dante brought
   To Beatrice; the sapphire Laura wore
When Petrarch cut it sparkling out of thought;
   The ruby Shakespeare hewed from his heart's core;
The dark, deep emerald that Rossetti wrought
   For his own soul, to wear for evermore.

                EUGENE LEE-HAMILTON.

Another Answer to the Same Question

What is a sonnet? 'Tis the pearly shell
   That murmurs of the far-off, murmuring sea;
   A precious jewel carved most curiously—
It is a little picture painted well.
What is a sonnet? 'Tis the tear that fell
   From a great poet's hidden ecstasy,
   A two-edged sword, a star, a song, ah, me!
Sometimes a heavy-tolling funeral bell.

This was the flame that shook with Dante's breath,
   The solemn organ whereon Milton played,
      And the clear glass where Shakspeare's shadow falls;
A sea this is—beware who ventureth!
   For like a fjord the narrow floor is laid
      Deep as mid ocean to the sheer mountain walls.

                RICHARD WATSON GILDER.

Written on a Blank Leaf in Mr. Samuel Waddington's 'Sonnets of Europe'

Now have I for the second time perused
   This little volume of translated rhymes,
   Gathered from many languages and climes,
And into English elegantly fused.
When sad, not seldom have I been amused
   By listening to the sonnet's silvery chimes;
   The sonnet which I love—though oftentimes
It be by clumsy hands like mine abused.

And though within this volume may be read
   Some sonnets well deserving of our praise,
   We have at home by far surpassed them all,
These foreign bards. Here Shakespeare's muse was bred;
   Here Wordsworth, Keats, Rossetti, wore the bays;
   Here Milton's sonnets rang like bugle-call.

THOMAS AULD.

Elixir

Pure form, that like some chalice of old time
   Contain'st the liquid of the poet's thought
   Within thy curving hollow, gem-enwrought
   With interwoven traceries of rhyme,
While o'er thy brim the bubbling fancies climb,
   What thing am I that undismayed have sought
   To pour my verse with trembling hand untaught
Into a shape so small yet so sublime?

Because perfection haunts the hearts of men,
   Because thy sacred chalice gathered up
   The wine of Petrarch, Shakspere, Shelley—then
Receive these tears of failure as they drop
   (Sole vintage of my life), since I am fain
   To pour them in a consecrated cup.

EDITH WHARTON.

To Petrarch

Pétrarque, au doux sonnet je fus longtemps rebelle,
Mais toi, divin Toscan, chaste et voluptueux,
Tu choisis, évitant tout rhythme impétueux,
Pour ta belle pensée une forme humble et belle.

Ton poème aujourd'hui par des charmes m'appelle :
Vase étroit mais bien clos, coffret plaisir des yeux,
D'où exhale un parfum subtil, mystérieux,
Que Laure respirait, le soir, dans la chapelle.

Aux souplesses de l'art ta grâce se plaisait ;
Maître, tu souriras si ma muse rurale
Et libre a fait ployer la forme magistrale ;

Puis, sur le tour léger de l'Etrusque, naissait,
Docile à varier la forme antique et sainte,
L'urne pour les parfums, ou le miel, ou l'absinthe.

Auguste Brizeux.

The same Imitated

Long time I scorned to wear the sonnet's yoke,
  Nor cared how featly 'neath its bondage played,
  Sweet amorist of the Valclusian shade,
Thy fancies chaste and tender. But they spoke
In witcheries so winning, I outbroke
  At last all zeal to swing the gem-inlaid
  Small thurible that stole, when Laura prayed,
Her thoughts from Heaven with delicate incense-smoke.

Thou wilt not frown, then, forehead crowned and starred,
  If on a rustic flute I fain would learn
To mimic thy Uranian tones. Unmarred
  Its type, thou sawest the Tuscan potter turn
No less for the wild thyme the classic urn
  Than for the musk or Indian spikenard.

George O'Neill, S.J.

A German Sonnet on the Sonnet

 Sonette dichtete mit edlem Feuer
Ein Mann, der willig trug der Liebe Kette.
Er sang sie der vergötterten Laurette,
Im Leben ihm und nach dem Leben theuer.

 Und also sang auch manches Abenteuer
In schmelzend musikalischem Sonette
Ein Held, der einst durch wildes Wogenbette
Mit seinem Liede schwamm, als seinem Steuer.

 Der Deutsche hat sich beigesellt, ein Dritter,
Dem Florentiner und dem Portugiesen,
Und sang geharnischte für kühne Ritter.

 Auf diese folg' ich, die sich gross erwiesen,
Nur wie ein Aehrenleser folgt dem Schnitter,
Denn nicht als Vierter wag' ich mich zu diesen.
   Augustus von Platen-Hallermünde.

The same Translated

Sonnets with noble fire he framed who bore
 Full willingly of Love the gentle chains.
 To worshipped Laura warbled he his strains,
Dear to his soul in life, in death still more.

The hero, too, who, shipwrecked, reached the shore
 With his great poem for his only helm,
 While the wild billows sought to overwhelm—
He many a melting sonnet did outpour.

The German who has chanted loud and free
 Sonnets in panoply for doughty knights
  Has joined the Florentine and Portuguese.
 Great as they are, I dare to follow these,
 But as a gleaner whom small gain requites,
Not as a fourth to such a mighty three.[1]
   The Editor.

---

[1] This sonnet refers to Petrarch, Camoens, and Rückert. Camoens when shipwrecked in the Gulf of Siam swam ashore with nothing but his poem, *The Lusiad*. Rückert in 1813 published his patriotic *Sonnets in Armour*.

Il Sonetto

Dante il mover gli diè del cherubino
E d' aere azzurro e d' or lo circonfuse :
Petrarca il pianto del suo cor, divino
Rio che pe' versi mormora, gl' infuse.

La mantuana ambrosia e 'l venosino
Miel gl' impetrò da le tiburti muse
Torquato ; e come strale adamantino
Contro i servi e tiranni Alfier lo schiuse.

La nota Ugo gli diè de' rusignoli
Sotto i ionii cipressi e dell' acanto
Cinsel fiorito a' suoi materni soli.

Sesto io no, ma postremo, estasi e pianto
E profumo, ira ed arte, a' miei dì soli
Memore innovo ed a i sepolcri canto.
      G. Carducci.

The same Translated

Dante gave movement to it as the flight
 Of cherubim through azure air and gold ;
 Petrarch the sorrows of his own heart told
In streams divine of murmuring music bright.
Sweetness of Mantua and Venusian dew
 The Muses gave to Tasso for its sake,
 While Alfieri's steel-tipped arrows rake
Tyrants and slaves, with scorn still whetted new.

Notes of the nightingale to it were given
 By Ugo 'mid Ionian cypresses,
Bound with acanthus 'neath his mother's heaven.[1]
 Sixth am I not but last ; remembering these,
I unto tombs in this my day have striven
 To sing plaints, wrath, art, sweetness, ecstasies.
      Charlotte Grace O'Brien.

---

[1] The island of Zante was the birthplace of Ugo Foscolo and of his mother.

Al Sonetto

Breve e amplissimo carme, o lievemente
Co 'l pensier volto a mondi altri migliori
L' Alighier ti profili, o te co' fiori
Colga il Petrarca lungo un rio corrente :
   Te pur vestia degli epici splendori
Prigion Torquato, e in aspre note e lente
Ti scolpia quella man che sì potente
Pugnò co' marmi a trarne vita fuori :
   A l' Eschil poi, che su l' Avon rinacque,
Tu, peregrin con l' arte a strania arena,
Fosti d' arcan dolori arcan richiamo :
   L' anglo e 'l lusiade Omero in te si piacque :
Ma Bavio, che i gran versi urlando sfrena,
Bavio t' odia, o sonetto : ond' io più t' amo.

G. Carducci.

The same Translated

Brief but most full art thou, O little song !
   If lightly pencilled by the hand of him,
   Dante, who looked on other worlds, or trim
With flowers that Petrarch plucked the streams along.
The prisoner Tasso's epic splendours fill
   Thy scanty space ; he who with art's long strife
   Wrought the rude marble into breathing life,
With harsh slow notes subdued thee to his will.
The Æschylus new-born in Avon's dell
   To thee a welcome pilgrim did rehearse
   Mysterious sorrows in mysterious verse ;
English and Lusiad Homers loved thee well—
   But Bavius, noisiest shrieker of the grove,
   Hates thee, O sonnet !—whence the more I love.[1]

Charlotte G. O'Brien.

---

[1] The seven poets indicated here are Dante, Petrarch, Tasso, Michael Angelo, Shakespeare, Milton and Camoens.

Another Version of the preceding Sonnet

Short but most spacious song, thee Dante drew
In dainty outline, as his thought took flight
To other better worlds ; thee Petrarch's sprite
Gather'd with flowers that by a river grew ;
'Twas thee imprisoned Tasso robed anew
With epic splendours ; and that hand of might
Which strove from marble to bring life to light,
Carved thee in notes, rugged and heavy too ;
Then to that Æschylus, new-born by Avon's leas,
With Art a pilgrim on a foreign strand,
Thou wert a secret voice for secret store :
Both Homers loved thee, English and Portuguese ;
But Bavius, who howls loose his verses grand
Hates thee, O sonnet,—so I love thee more.
    EDWARD BURROUGH BROWNLOW (1857-1895).

A JOSÉPHIN SOULARY

Vous êtes le fin ciseleur !
Vous prenez un burin de flamme,
Et vous faites un amalgame
De la forme et de la couleur.

Le sonnet, ce calice en fleur,
Jaillit du creuset de votre âme ;
Vous y burinez tout le drame
De l'amour et de la douleur.

Avec art votre esprit découpe
Le penser dont les vers se font :
L'œuvre rit, chatoie, et se groupe ;

Puis, tenant le vase profond,
Comme Cléopâtre en sa coupe,
Vous jetez une perle au fond !
    PROSPER BLANCHEMAIN.

The Academy of the Sonnet[1]

Poème-colibri qu'épargne la critique,
Avec cette clef d'or Shakspeare ouvre son cœur,
Sur ce doux luth Pétrarque enchante sa douleur,
Et le Tasse captif se calme à sa musique.

Dante mêle ce myrte à son laurier magique,
Michel Ange amoureux cultive cette fleur,
Camoëns de ce rhythme a connu la douceur,
Et Milton l'ennoblit d'un accent héroïque.

A nos rimeurs gaulois cette forme plaisait ;
Depuis le vieux Ronsard jusqu'à toi, Sainte-Beuve,
La Muse de la France à ce ruisseau s'abreuve !

Citerai-je Barbier, Laprade, Autran, Musset ?
Enfin, grâce au concours d'une pléiade amie,
Le sonnet en Provence a son Académie.
Comte Lafond.

French Masters

J'aime un sonnet sonnant, brillant, prime-sautier,
Comme en faisaient jadis Maynard et Maleville ;
Comme en faisaient encore hier, dans notre ville,
Arvers et Soulary, Sainte-Beuve et Gautier.

J'aime à lire un sonnet, j'aime à le déguster
Lentement, savamment et sur chaque papille,
Comme fait d'un vin vieux le connaisseur habile
Qu'on voit se recueillir pour mieux se délecter.

L'esprit dans un sonnet, c'est un vin tout aimable
Qui du cerveau jaillit, mousseux et rubicon,
Et qu'on trouve meilleur dans un petit flacon.

Mais hélas ! qu'ai-je dit ? . . . Mon dieu ! je suis capable
D'attaquer les buveurs.—Mon flacon n'est pas grand,
Et cependant mon vin est loin d'être énivrant.
Irma Méray.

[1] This is explained in our Preface.

A Evariste Boulay-Paty

Il est contrée où la France est bacchante,
Où la liqueur de feu mûrit au grand soleil,
Où des volcans éteints frémit la cendre ardente,
Où l'esprit des vins purs aux laves est pareil.

Là, près d'un chêne assis sous la vigne pendante,
Des livres préférés j'assemble le conseil ;
Là, l'octave du Tasse, le tercet de Dante,
Me chantent l'Angelus à l'heure du réveil.

De ces deux chants naquit le sonnet séculaire.
J'y pensais, comparant nos Français au Toscan ;
Vos sonnets sont venus parler au solitaire.

Je les aime et les roule, ainsi qu'un talisman
Qu'on tourne dans ses doigts, comme le doux rosaire,
Le chapelet sans fin du santon musulman.
ALFRED DE VIGNY (1799–1863).

The same Translated

Here in the South, where Mother France doth revel
  A Bacchant 'mid her vines, drinking a wild
  Volcanic soul from lava-hills that child
A fierier grape than Alicante or Seville,
Dwell I, an anchorite from noise of evil,
  And hear my daily Angelus ring mild
  From Dante's tercet and the octave filed
Of Tasso, when the morning rays fall level.

And as I marked their wedded rhythm mould
The sonnet's music, then, 'mid songs of old,
  Your sonnets dropped into my solitude.
  Ever I turn, re-turn them—in the wood
Or by the lamp, as the prayer-beads are told
  By child of Mary, or of false Mahmoud.
GEORGE O'NEILL, S. J.

IV.

THE SONNET'S LATEST VOTARIES

'A halting sonnet of his own pure brain.'

Much Ado about Nothing, v. 4

[The sonnets in this division, and many of the others, especially the translated sonnets, appeared in *The Irish Monthly*, and are now collected for the first time]

He was gone a long time, and Apollo, meanwhile,
Went over some sonnets of his with a file,
For, of all compositions, he thought that the sonnet
Best repaid all the toil you expended upon it ;
It should reach with one impulse the end of its course,
And for one final blow collect all its force ;
Not a verse should be salient, but each one should tend
With a wavelike upgathering to break at the end ;
So, condensing the strength here, there smoothing a wrinkle,
He was killing the time, &c.
     RUSSELL LOWELL'S *Fable for Critics*.

A Sonnet on the Sonnet

The first line of a sonnet is a door
   Into a room from Fancy's entrance hall;
   A little room, so narrow that the wall
Just holds one picture from the tenant's store.
Yet see! 'tis but a mirror set before
   The window pane, and as you turn to find
   What made the frame so meet and you so blind,
You gaze on verities he loves still more.

For towards the end he throws the window wide
   To win a glimpse of beauty's seeds upspringing
Trim paths of pleasantness that need no guide,
   Where to Truth's stem imagination's clinging
Like ivy;—till you fain would fare outside,
   For overhead you hear the heavens are singing.

                      MOSSE MACDONALD.

Through the Lattice

Securely, through the sonnet's fourteen bars
   As from a lattice, Poesy looks down,
   While other citadels of song are blown
Into the dust with every wind that wars.
No storms assail her here, no fashion mars:
   Immortal wreaths have round her casement grown
   Through which she marks our human smile and frown,
Or lifts a pensive gaze to holy stars.

O Poesy, be ever safe immured
   Here where the mightiest have paused to sing,
      And fledgling bards lisped forth their waking note;
And, haply to thy cloister-prison lured,
   May flights of music stay a wandering wing,
      As once of old in Barbara's tower remote.

                      ELINOR SWEETMAN.

A Woman's Sonnet

'And could a woman, think you, be content
  With laws so many and with words so few?
  Methinks more licence she would deem her due
Ere half her wealth of eloquence were spent.'
Nay, sir, a woman's neck is early bent
  Beneath some yoke, more trammelled far than *you*,
  She murmurs not if fain to stoop anew
And don these jingling chains by muses lent.

Unchecked the man his inmost heart reveals,
  That all the world may know his hopes and fears,
    His loves or sorrows are his favourite themes;
But none must guess what suffering woman feels
  Who hides with joyless smiles her need of tears.
    Her, then, the sonnet's reticence beseems.

                      M. E. Francis.

A Father's Sonnet

A babble of happy murmurs, like a brook's :
A joy that blossoms from the heart of sorrow :
A little hand that leads us, rushing thorough,
To Nature, from the ashen track of books :
Remembrance, smiting with the tend'rest looks :
A voice of Faith in faithless wildernesses :
A love, in hermit-cell, that only blesses,
Unknowing the world's silence or rebukes.
God's smile, that haloes innocence : a breath
Divine, to one who climbs the pit of death :
The sword of flame of the Angel o' the Sun,
Rifting the night : dew in the lily's cup,
Blending of earth and heaven.
                      Do these make up
The sonnet?   Then my year-old babe is one.

                    George Noble Plunkett.

Soul and Body

A sonnet is the body of a thought,
   Which enters suddenly the poet's mind
   And breathes its way, mysterious as the wind,
Unrecognised, as first it was unsought.
Whilst yet unformed, 'tis kindred to the nought
   Whence it arose ; the poet still must find
   Some spirit-worthy shape in which to bind
The subtle life wherewith his mind is fraught.

A stanza rises from the mental deep,
   Rhymes well disposed, with rhythm of even flow ;
     Full use of sense, due length of limb it gives,
A body fit. The thought aroused from sleep,
   Flushes the rhythm with a poetic glow,
     And in the sonnet's form for ever lives.

FREDERICK C. KOLBE, D.D.

Ros in Rosa

A sonnet should be like a dewdrop, round,
   Full-orbed, and lucid ; nestled in one flower,
   And, of the myriad blossoms of the hour,
Reflecting but the beauty it has crown'd.
It should have fallen from heaven, nor from the ground
   Have taken birth, although the sheltering bower
   Be decked and fair with Eden's long-lost dower
Wherein its sphere of life be duly found.
   And, as the dew repeats the sky's grey morn
     In tender monotone, or in the sun's full light
Catches afire, and burns with prism'd ray,
   So should the sonnet, thus divinely born,
     With many-coloured meaning still be bright,
Changing, as man's mood changeth, day by day.

ALICE F. BARRY.

A Willing Slave

I love to be 'cribbed, cabined, and confined'
   Within the sonnet's fourteen lines of space ;
   To me it seems the beau-ideal of grace,
Into its limits to compress the mind.
Though some assert its narrow boundaries bind
   And stop the flow of thought's untiring pace,
   I would not add a line, nor one erase—
To mar a feature that the gods designed.

'A thing of beauty' 'tis, wherein the soul
   Finds blest enchantment, glorious, divine,
   With all the witchery that enthralled the Nine ;
No wonder, then, that *all* its charms extol—
And that free praise is ever vented on it,
Soft, soothing, stately, sweet, seductive sonnet !

CHARLES F. FORSHAW.

A Set of Similes

The sonnet is a diamond flashing round
   From every facet true rare-coloured lights ;
   A gem of thought carved in poetic nights
To grace the brow of art by fancy crowned ;
A miniature of soul, wherein are found
   Marvels of beauty and resplendent sights ;
   A drop of blood with which a lover writes
His heart's sad epitaph in its own bound :

A pearl gained from dark waters when the deep
   Rocked in its frenzied passion ; the last note
   Heard from a heaven-saluting skylark's throat ;
A cascade small flung in a canyon steep
   With crystal music. At this shrine of song
   High priests of poesy have worshipped long.

EDWARD BURROUGH BROWNLOW.

The Oneness of the Sonnet

Into the bare, scant chamber of my mind
   Once came a single thought,—full rare a guest,—
   Mantled with deep mantilla from eye's quest;
Whom to detain I artfully combined
A measured melody, two rhymes entwined;
   Her play with which let 'scape her beauty's best,
   Then hoped I she'd lay open all the rest,—
Ah! tired of toys, she cast them to the wind.

There was a pause; these I, by subtle spell,
   In trinity of new rhymes deftly wrought
   To longer lapsing rhythm, must eclipse!
The fantasy, I ween, was conjured well,
   For, in delight at having them, my Thought
   Unveiling, sprang, a sonnet, to my lips.

                D. MONCRIEFF O'CONNOR.

The Sonnet of a Lifetime

Shaped like the sonnet, would my soul might build
   The story of itself, where all might read
   Complete development through word and deed
Of one great purpose that had fed and filled
Its orb and outline; as a man, well-skilled
   In cameo-carving, though the shell impede,
   Cuts crisp the clear brows of one born to lead
His fellows, since firm-thoughted and straight-willed:

So, rounded surely to a perfect close,
   And steeped in music, life with its own end
      Might crown itself, as the declining day's
Crown is the crimson sunset when it goes.
   Such life, four-square, needs nothing to commend,
      Being itself beyond both price and praise.

                JOHN KANE.

The Laws of the Sonnet

A perfect sonnet fails not to confine
   The metre strictly to its rule of rhyme :
   Throughout the quatrains, in well ordered time,
   Two rhymes alone their harmony combine.

These in two ways the sonnet may entwine—
   Such the fixed rule in its own Southern clime—
   Either the two alternately may chime,
   Or else a couplet link each central line.

Where ends each quatrain, pause, and pause again
   Between the tercets ; these, as suits it best,
   Your pen may finish with two rhymes or three.

Take heed your tercets ne'er by chance contain
   A couplet :—carelessly these rules transgress'd,
   Your fourteen lines will no true sonnet be.
       R. E. EGERTON-WARBURTON (1804–1891).

The Sonnet's Solace

When the heart presses hard against its bars,
And all the aching senses seek to reach,
Through some determinate sweet form of speech,
A rest and outcome from their inward jars ;
The sonnet then across our brain's mad wars
Draws near to us as some soft-handed leech,
Giving our thoughts deliverance, setting each
Free and alone, self-centred as the stars.
Soon to these new-born things new beauties come,
And earth and air and all the sky and sea
Bring tribute to them of sweet minstrelsy,
So sweet, the cry within the heart is dumb ;
And where was pain as of a love unsought
Is now a fount of ever living thought.
       CHARLOTTE GRACE O'BRIEN.

The Complete Sonneteer

To make a sonnet write your first line out ;
Construct your second upon any theme,
The third comes easily into the scheme,
The fourth you welcome with a joyful shout,
The fifth comes readily enough about,
The sixth rhymes with the second, keep up steam,
The seventh and the third make up a team,
And now the eighth is right, beyond a doubt.

Now cannot any man do just as much ?
To pick the words is not so great a task,
And though he lack the fine ethereal touch
If in the Muses' smile he may not bask,
He still may get the sonnet form, and such
Is all that you can reasonably ask.
JOHN E. NORCROSS.

Sonnets by Rule

Two stanzas in heroic measure try
In which the rhymes shall be the same, and then,
It is but pastime for the fluent pen,
The fourth line written ere the first is dry.
It is no effort, and you need not pry
For old book-words ; take those of common ken,
The daily speech of ordinary men,
The costermonger's shout, the newsboy's cry.

Still six lines more, in couplets or in threes :
The tale is short, and words are plenty now,
They hover round, and you have but to seize
And fit them into place ; then calm your brow :
A sonnet you can write with perfect ease
Upon this model, if you but know how.
JOHN E. NORCROSS.

The Sonnet

Weird Paganini from a single string
  Drew melodies that held the heart in thrall ;
  To mediocrity the stage seems small,
Yet Siddons to its mimic world did bring
Genius, that raised it to a mighty thing,
  Stirring men's blood to tumult ; mark the call
  Of that shy bird, the cuckoo, rise and fall—
Two notes suffice to give a voice to spring.

  It is the power, the passion, and the fire
    That elevate the form. The wind can sigh
As deftly through a chink as where the spoil
Of autumn smoulders on earth's funeral pyre.
  A pebble carved by Phidias would outvie
A mountain reared by some poor plodder's toil.

T. H. Wright.

The Dry Bones of a Sonnet

Thyself, O sonnet ! thy strict laws expound.
  Twice seven heroic lines, five rhymes, at most,
  Whereof my octave but one pair should boast,
Like *In Memoriam* stanzas interwound.
The eighth line duly turned, the muse is bound
  To pause, as if with anxious thought engrossed,
  How to land safely on the nearing coast,
For here her little skiff may run aground.

Six lines remain. 'Tis best these lines to enlace
  In sloping tercets—three new rhymes at first,
    Receding inward from the margin so.
Lastly, three corresponding rhymes we place
  In order similar or just reversed.
    Yet genius 'neath such gyves can soar and glow !

M. R.

Sonnet Laws Self-Expounded

A sonnet is built up of lines fourteen,
   Each with five beats; whereof the first eight rest
   Contented with two rhymes—at least 'tis best
To share a single rhyming sound between
Lines two and three, six, seven : although, I ween,
   The second quatrain may, if sorely pressed
   To turn its middle couplet thus, request
Leave to produce a third rhyme on the scene.

After this octave, pause; then start anew
   With two fresh rhymes, alternately combined,
Or with three rhymes arranged in order due—
   In the first tercet separate rhymes we find,
And in the last, three corresponding, too,
   But oft with order opposite assigned.

                                          M. R.

Sonnet Mechanism

Fourteen ten-syllabled iambic lines
   Rhymed in two quatrains thus : *a, b, b, a.*
   Such is the classical Petrarchan way,
But usage in our harsher tongue inclines
To wider tolerance, and oft assigns
   A third rhyme for the middle couplet here,
   Where to its close the octave draweth near
And for a breathing-space the poet pines.

The sestet follows with its two new rhymes,
   Alternate thus : *c d, c d, c d;*
More oft these tercets run in triple chimes,
   Of which the symbol is twice *c d e,*
Unless the closing tercet should betimes
   Reverse this order into *e d c.*

                                          M. R.

A Hundredth Defence of the Sonnet

The silly sneers which flippant critics fling
  Against the genuine sonnet's rigid laws
  Might be directed with as valid cause
'Gainst ev'ry rill from the Pierian spring.
All metre is a mystery. We sing
  God and His works in lines of measured length,
  And this mechanical device adds strength
To thoughts which else might drag a broken wing.

Stanza and rhyme—how can such childish art
  Avail to move the spiritual soul?
    Why not left free to choose best words that come?
    These magic bands no bondage are to some;
  They but exert a wholesome, wise control,
And through the ear more surely reach the heart.

M. R.

A Typewriter's Sonnet

A solemn moment this when first my Muse
  The typoscriptor's magic keys hath pressed!
  Unskilled as yet to work her full behest,
But still a sonnet she will ne'er refuse.
The happy instrument she deigns to choose
  Is No 2 of Remington—the best,
  As far as one may judge to whom the rest
Are as unknown as is to-morrow's news.

O Remingtonian Number Two! be thou
  Henceforth the medium to enrich mankind
    With plenteous prose and very scanty rhyme.
But lo! we've reached the closing tercet now,
  And in this dainty casket lies enshrined
    My first type-written sonnet for all time.

M. R.

A Magazine of Sonnets

Of all the Journals that the world hath seen
   Each week or month these hundred years and more,
   Not one a richer harvest ever bore
Of sonnets than our own dear Magazine
Yclept 'The Irish Monthly.' Has there been
   In Journals thrice its size such lavish store?
   A single number sometimes pays its score—
Not all home-made, but quite enough, I ween.

Though Genius and the Muse must still be free,
   A sterner policy shall now be tried,
     For Maga has herself too truly said:
'Of Magazines that have been or shall be,'
   (Is this the blush of shame or smirk of pride?)
     'Behold in me the most besonneted.'[1]

                      M. R.

'So easy not to Write'

'It is so easy *not* to write a sonnet!'
   As Mr. Andrew Lang doth oft complain;
   And yet of men apparently quite sane
How many seem to set their hearts upon it!
This tiny foolscap, scores of rhymesters don it
   As eagerly as in Fourth William's reign
   Our grandmothers (then chits of girls) were fain
To don their very newest Leghorn bonnet.

A sonnet is so easy not to write!
   Thus let them cry who ne'er have written one.
But what about the wretched, wilful wight
   Who thinks his little head contains a ton
Of teeming fancies yearning for the light?
   But this is line fourteen, and I have done.

                      M. R.

---

[1] This confession regards 'The Irish Monthly' of some ten years ago. In 1887 seventy-six sonnets were printed in its pages, of which forty-five were original. The supply of sonnets has since been rigidly restricted.

SOLATIOLUM

I count me blest in tranquil tastes that fill
   Right pleasantly my being's nooks and corners.
   E'en since these thumbs were tiny as Jack Horner's,
Such tastes have comforted and comfort still.
Did they but while an hour away not ill,
   It were enough to screen them from the scorners;
   But gilders they, refiners and adorners
Of Life's not always palatable pill.

Sonnet aroon, *thou* hast been one of those.
   Full many a vivid moment have I spent
     In smoothing out thy octave's dual measure:
Until by contrast it seemed easy prose
   To let thy tercets follow their own bent,
     Masking obedience as the whim of pleasure.

                              M. R.

AN OLD MAN'S SONNET

The youthful heart affects the vague, the vast,
   And shrinks from the complete and definite;
   The wise constraint of order seems for it
Like the close cage that holds the linnet fast.
And hence their thoughts young poets rarely cast
   In mould amenable to sonnet-laws—
   That subtle symmetry of rhyme and pause,
Which makes the jewel-thought flash out at last.

But we for whom Life's sonnet glides away
   Through its last ebbing tercet—*we* are fain
     To be by metric manacles restrained.
Some briefer task befits our waning day:
   An epic feat would unachieved remain,
     But lo! in course so short the goal is quickly gained.

                              M. R.

A JEWELLED SHRINE

As when in some dim jewel-crusted shrine,
A maze of shaft and scroll-work, swings on high
A lamp whose gleams, flooding the glories nigh,
Leave vistas vaguely rich ; around it shine
Responsive sparks of brilliance opaline
That down the scented dusk melt, glow, and die—
Tint chasing tint in soft light harmony—
As seems the flame, faint-stirred, to wax or pine :
So in the sonnet, where the hoarded treasure
Of poet's mind lies hidden, where is wrought
By heart and brain, as fire and hammer, nought
But strong and graceful, welded truth and pleasure—
How brightly answer beauties beyond measure
The flash of fancy in this shrine of thought !

JOSEPH KEATING, S. J.

SONNETS OF LIFE

I. YOUTH

What is a sonnet ? 'Tis a leaping brook
   That sings a short but joyous melody
   From its near fountain to the unknown sea
Where it shall find the old haunts it forsook,
Sun-drawn, upon the garish earth to look
   One brief, forgetful day ; perpetually
   Bidding farewells without a pang, to be
The momentary guest of some fresh nook.

Thus, drawn from deeps of the eternal years,
   Our slender life-tide careless leaps along,
Bidding farewells for ever, without tears,
   To the embracing banks we pass among,
Until again the unknown deep appears—
   And ends the sonnet, hushes the short song.

II. AGE

What is a sonnet ?   'Tis a twilight sea
   Ebbing and flowing to the rhythmic tune
   Of hollow-sounding shores whose soft bassoon
Seems but to deepen silence and set free
Ghosts of dead tumults—prisoned fearfully
   In multitudinous clamours of the noon—
   Visiting now the glimpses of the moon
And rustling the solitude with melody.

Thus, in the twilight hour ere life depart,
   Alone will memory's chord, vibrating slow,
Make sonnet-music with my sluggish heart,
   Rhythming my pulse to solemn ebb and flow :
Yet in its midst—what myriad ghosts will start
   From mouldering cerements of the Long Ago !

III. L'ENVOI

A sonnet ?   'Tis the reed through which we blow
   A shepherd's ditty ; or the sharp command
   Of stern-faced duty ; or an anthem grand—
Pipings of pleasure, or a wail of woe.
A sonnet ?   'Tis the clay, plastic as dough,
   Moulded to meanest uses by the hand
   Of some dull artisan ; or, artist-planned,
'Tis named ' Praxiteles ! ' or ' Angelo ! '

Our life—is it a listless wind-blown reed,
   Meet instrument for wanton mirth of Pan ?
Our life—is it the clay we careless knead—
   Hushing *I will*, to hear alone *I can* ?
O friend ! your life's a sonnet—short, indeed :
   Make it an anthem, and yourself a man !

HUGH T. HENRY.

V.

THE SONNET'S KINDRED SELF-DESCRIBED

'Those old French ways of verse-making that have been coming into fashion of late—surely they say a pretty thing more prettily for their quaint old-fashioned liberty! That triolet—how deliciously impertinent it is! is it not? . . . The variety of dainty modes wherein by shape and sound a very pretty something is carved out of nothing at all. Their fantastic surprises, the ring of their bell-like returns upon themselves, their music of triangle and cymbal. In some of them poetry seems to approach the nearest possible to bird-song—to unconscious seeming through most unconscious art, imitating the carelessness and impromptu of forms as old as the existence of birds, and as new as every fresh individual joy in each new generation, growing their own feathers, and singing their own song, yet always the feathers of their kind, and the song of their kind.'

GEORGE MACDONALD.

A Rondeau on the Rondeau

Ma foi, c'est fait de moi, car Isabeau
M'a conjuré de lui faire un rondeau.
Cela me met en une peine extrême :
Quoi ! treize vers, huit en *eau*, cinq en *ème* !
Je lui ferais aussitôt un bateau.

En voilà cinq pourtant en un monceau.
Faisons-en huit en invoquant Brodeau,
Et puis mettons, par quelque stratagème :
    Ma foi, c'est fait.

Si je pouvais encor de mon cerveau
Tirer cinq vers, l'ouvrage serait beau ;
Mais cependant je suis dedans l'onzième :
Et ci je crois que je fais le douzième :
En voilà treize ajustés au niveau.
    Ma foi, c'est fait.
        VOITURE (1598–1648).

The same Imitated

You bid me try, BLUE-EYES, to write
A rondeau. What ! forthwith ?—To-night ?
  Reflect. Some skill I have, 'tis true ;
  But thirteen lines !—and rhymed on two !—
'Refrain,' as well. Ah, hapless plight !

Still there are five lines—ranged aright.
These Gallic bonds, I feared, would fright
  My easy Muse. They did, till you—
    You bid me try !

That makes them eight. The port's in sight :
'Tis all because your eyes are bright !
  Now just a pair to end in 'oo'—
  When maids command, what can't we do !
Behold ! the RONDEAU, tasteful, light,
    You bid me try !
        AUSTIN DOBSON.

My First Rondeau

My first rondeau, this is the hour
Predestined to behold thee flower,
   Thy petals opening without flaw,
   Obedient to a hidden law,
Like spring's young leaves in sun and shower.

Whence cometh the mysterious power
Which doth sounds deftly ordered dower?
   Whose were the happy eyes that saw
        The first rondeau?

Now art thou rounded, like a tower
O'erhanging some fair garden bower;
   Yet thou, like nobler works, shalt fa'
   Into oblivion's ravening maw:
For instance, *who* now reads 'The Giaour,'
        My first rondeau?

              THE EDITOR.

My Last Rondeau

My dying hour, how near art thou?
Or near or far, my head I bow
   Before God's ordinance supreme;
   But ah, how priceless then will seem
Each moment rashly squandered now!

Teach me, for thou canst teach me, how
These fleeting instants to endow
   With worth that may the past redeem,
        My dying hour!

My barque, that late with buoyant prow
The sunny waves did gaily plough,
   Now through the sunset's fading gleam
   Drifts dimly shoreward in a dream.
I feel the land-breeze on my brow,
        My dying hour!

              THE EDITOR.

The Rondeau

First find your refrain—then build as you go
With delicate touch, neither heavy nor slow,
  But dainty and light as a gossamer thread,
  Or the fleecy white cloud that is breaking o'erhead,
Or the sea-foam that curls in the soft evening glow ;
And your rhyme must be swinging—not all in a row,
But as waves on the sands in fine ebb and quick flow ;
  Yet of rules for a rondeau I hold this the head,
        First find your refrain.

For the subject—there's nothing above or below
That a poet can learn or a critic may know
  But a rondeau will hold a rhyme-ring that will wed
  The thought to the thing ; yet whatever is said
Will ne'er be a rondeau till you with one blow
        First find your refrain.

                E. B. Brownlow.

An Unpunctuated Villanelle

[The dictionary says a villanelle consists of nineteen lines on two rhymes arranged in six stanzas, the first five of three lines, the last of four. The first and third of the first stanza are repeated alternately as last lines from the second to the fifth stanza, and then conclude the sixth stanza. The dictionary adds that it is difficult to make the lines fit in with sense. It is.]

    When first I read a villanelle
      I could not understand a word
    Such rigours in its numbers dwell

    And what I said I will not tell
      For I am glad that no one heard
    When first I read a villanelle

    In sheer despair I gave a yell
      I did although it seems absurd
    Such rigours in its numbers dwell

With lexicons I broke its spell
   And found the meaning was deferred
When first I read a villanelle

The pride by which an angel fell
   In such attempt might be deterred
Such rigours in its numbers dwell

And now I know that it was well
   That that which did should have occurred
When first I read a villanelle
Such rigours in its numbers dwell

[*I decline to punctuate.*—H.M-B., *in Westminster Gazette.*]

A Villanelle on the Villanelle

A dainty thing's a villanelle.
   Sly, musical, a jewel in rhyme
It serves its purpose passing well.

A double-clappered silver bell
   That must be made to clink in chime,
A dainty thing's the villanelle;

And if you wish to flute a spell,
   Or ask a meeting 'neath the lime,
It serves its purpose passing well.

You must not ask of it the swell
   Of organs grandiose and sublime—
A dainty thing's the villanelle;

And, filled with sweetness, as a shell
   Is filled with sound, and launched in time,
It serves its purpose passing well.

Still fair to see and good to smell,
   As in the quaintness of its prime,
A dainty thing's the villanelle,
It serves its purpose passing well.

                  W. E. Henley.

How to compose a Villanelle

It's all a trick, quite easy when you know it,
   As easy as reciting A B C ;
You need not be an atom of a poet.

If you've a grain of wit and want to show it,
   Writing a villanelle—take this from me—
It's all a trick, quite easy when you know it.

You start a pair of rhymes, and then you 'go it'
   With rapid-running pen and fancy free ;
You need not be an atom of a poet.

Take any thought, write round it or below it,
   Above or near it, as it liketh thee—
It's all a trick, quite easy when you know it.

Pursue your task, till, like a shrub, you grow it
   Up to the standard size it ought to be ;
You need not be an atom of a poet.

Clean it of weeds and water it and hoe it,
   Then watch it blossom with triumphant glee.
It's all a trick, quite easy when you know it ;
You need not be an atom of a poet.

WALTER SKEAT.

Pour faire une Villanelle

Pour faire une villanelle,
   Rime en 'elle' et rime en 'in,'
La méthode est simple et belle.

On dispose en kyrielle
   Cinq tercets, plus un quatrain,[1]
Pour faire une villanelle.

---

[1] The poet defends this rule in prose : 'Plus, ce serait trop. On mettrait du plomb aux ailes de ce léger poème.'

Sur le premier vers en *elle*
  Le second tercet prend fin :
La méthode est simple et belle.

Le troisième vers fidèle,
  Alterne comme refrain
Pour faire une villanelle.

La ronde ainsi s'entremêle ;
  L'un, puis l'autre, va son train ;
La méthode est simple et belle.

La dernière ritournelle
  Les voit se donner la main :
Pour faire une villanelle,
La méthode est simple et belle.

JOSEPH BOULMIER.

The same Translated

To make a tripping villanelle,
  With rhyme in *el*, and rhyme in *ain*,
A simple method will serve well.

The poet takes (his trick I tell)
  But five tercets and one quatrain
To make a tripping villanelle.

Upon the first verse with its *el*
  The second tercet ends amain ;
A simple method will serve well.

The third verse like a choral bell
  Alternates aptly as refrain
To make a tripping villanelle.

The tercets thus in sound and swell
  Swift follow in each other's train,
A simple method will serve well.

The quatrain like a sentinel
  Takes care the rhymes clasp hands again.
To make a tripping villanelle,
A simple method will serve well.
JAMES BOWKER.

How a Roundel is wrought

A roundel is wrought as a ring or a starbright sphere,
With craft of delight and with cunning of sound unsought,
That the heart of the hearer may smile if to pleasure
  his ear
    A roundel is wrought.

Its jewel of music is carven of all or of aught—
Love, laughter, or mourning—remembrance of rapture
  or fear—
That fancy may fashion to hang in the ear of thought.

As a bird's quick song runs round, and the hearts in us
  hear—
Pause answers to pause, and again the same strain caught,
So moves the device whence, round as a pearl or tear,
    A roundel is wrought.
ALGERNON C. SWINBURNE.

A Ballad of a Ballad

A sunset of purple and gold,
  Seen afar from the cliff's dizzy height;
A pageant of billows, that rolled
  In the glory of evening bedight :—
'Twas a picture indeed to invite
  My muse with an effort to strain
Her wings for a loftier flight—
  I never will venture again.

I searched through the singers of old
   For a metre, both graceful and bright;
I consulted my friends, and was told
   That the ballad was suitable quite.
I tried, and conceive my delight,
   When, choosing a nimble refrain,
I did the first stanza aright—
   I never will venture again.

Verse one was a joy to behold,
   A pleasure to read or recite,
'Twas a dainty melodious and bold
   Commingling of sweetness and light:
But the second—Ah! pity my plight!
   The rhymes were all used, and in vain
I struggled the whole of a night—
   I never will venture again.

Envoy

My friend, may you ne'er be cajoled
   Into metre, if haply your brain
Isn't cast in a metrical mould—
   I never will venture again.

                      C. J. STEWART.

Old French Forms

Of all the songs that dwell
   Where softest speech doth flow,
Some love the sweet rondel,
   And some the bright rondeau,
   With rhymes that tripping go,
In mirthful measures clad;
   But would I choose them?—No;
For me the blithe ballade!

O'er some, the villanelle,
  That sets the heart aglow,
Doth its enchanting spell,
  With lines recurring, throw ;
  Some, weighed with wasteful woe,
Gay triolets make them glad ;
  But would I choose them ?—No ;
For me the blithe ballade !

On chant of stately swell
  With measured feet and slow,
As grave as minster bell
  At vesper tolling slow,
  Do some their praise bestow ;
Some on sestinas sad ;
  But would I choose them ?—No ;
For me the blithe ballade !

Prince, to these songs a-row
  The Muse might endless add ;
But would I choose them ?—No ;
  For me the blithe ballade !

CLINTON SCOLLARD.

A RONDELET ON THE RONDELET

A rondelet
Is just seven verses rhymed on two.
  A rondelet
Is an old jewel quaintly set
In poesy—a drop of dew
Caught in a roseleaf. Lo ! for you
  A rondelet.

CHARLES HENRY LUDERS.

Un bon Triolet

Pour construire un bon triolet
   Il faut observer ces trois choses ;
Savoir, que l'air en soit folet ;
   Pour construire un bon triolet,
Qu'il rentre bien dans le rôlet,
   Et qu'il tombe au vrai lieu des pauses.
Pour construire un bon triolet
   Il faut observer ces trois choses.

St-Amand.

A Triolet on the Triolet

Easy is the triolet
   If you really learn to make it !
Once a neat refrain you get,
Easy is the triolet.
As you see !—I pay my debt
   With another rhyme. Deuce take it,
Easy is the triolet,
   If you really learn to make it.

Walter E. Henley.

Another

'Tis such a lovely little thing,
   This dancing, glancing triolet—
As light as swallows on the wing,
'Tis such a lovely little thing,
As bright as noonday skies in spring,
   As sweet as April's violet—
'Tis such a lovely little thing
   This dancing, glancing triolet.¶

Stonyhurst Magazine.

Apology for the Triolet

As a gleaming white pearl in its shell
  Lies the thought or the wish in the triolet.
'Tis as slight, but 'tis precious as well
As a gleaming white pearl in its shell,
Or the note of a silvern bell
  Or the scent of a springing violet.
As a gleaming white pearl in its shell,
  Lies the thought or the wish in the triolet.

Inigo Patrick Deane (1860–1895).

My First and Last Triolets

To M. V. R.

I

A triolet oh! let me try
  In honour of May Violet;
For violets are sweet and shy
(A triolet oh! let me try),
'And so,' quoth saucy May, 'am I!'—
  Fit theme for saucy triolet.
A triolet oh! let me try
  In honour of May Violet.

II

Though a rhyme your sweet name doth provide,
  This will certainly be my last triolet.
It is only the second I've tried,
Though a rhyme your sweet name doth provide.
An angel keeps guard at your side:
  Be by name and by nature a violet.
Though a rhyme your sweet name doth provide,
  This will certainly be my last triolet.

The Editor.

The Song

The song is as the thrush's note,
  Free, unpremeditated, strong.
On its own wave its form doth float,
  By its own breeze 'tis borne along.

'Tis but one impulse of the mind,
  Not overweighed with complex thought —
The wayward Spirit of the Wind
  In brief, impassioned measure caught.

T. H. WRIGHT.

A Quatrain on the Quatrain

Hark at the lips of this pink whorl of shell,
  And you shall hear the ocean's surge and roar;
So in the quatrain's measure, written well,
  A thousand lines shall all be sung in four.

FRANK DEMPSTER SHERMAN.

Hexameter and Pentameter Self-Described

Der epische Hexameter.

Schwindelnd trägt er dich fort auf rastlos strömenden Wogen;
Hinter dir siehst du, du siehst vor dir nur Himmel und Meer.

SCHILLER (1759–1805).

The Hexameter

Strongly it bears us along in swelling and limitless billows,
Nothing before and nothing behind but the sky and the ocean.

> *Translated by* COLERIDGE.

Das Distichon.

Im Hexameter steight des Springquells flüssige Säule;
Im Pentameter drauf fällt sie melodisch herab.

> SCHILLER.

The Elegiac Couplet

In the hexameter rises the fountain's silvery column,
In the pentameter aye falling in melody back.

> *Translated by* COLERIDGE.

Longfellow's Elegiacs

Peradventure of old, some bard in Ionian Islands,
  Walking alone by the sea, hearing the wash of the waves,
Learned the secret from them of the beautiful verse elegiac,
  Breathing into his song motion and sound of the sea.

For as the wave of the sea, upheaving in long undulations,
  Plunges loud on the sands, pauses, and turns, and retreats,
So the hexameter, rising and singing, with cadence sonorous,
  Falls; and in refluent rhythm back the pentameter flows.

Hexameter and Pentameter

I

In hexameter plunges the headlong cataract downward;
In pentameter up whirls the eddying mist.

II

In hexameter rolls sonorous the peal of the organ;
In pentameter soft rises the chant of the choir.

III

In hexameter gallops delighted a beggar on horseback;
In pentameter, whack! tumbles he off of his steed.

LONGFELLOW.

Other Metres Self-Described

ANAPÆST

When the Muse tells her story with galloping haste,
She will choose for her measure the brisk anapæst.

AMPHIBRACHS

But when elegiac and sad she doth wax,
She chooses iambics, not these amphibrachs.

IAMBICS

For grave iambics keep one steady pace,
With stress of voice on every second place.

TROCHEES

But the trochee, light and supple,
Strikes the first of ev'ry couple.

M. R.

SONNET PRINCIPLES

The sonnet is beginning to take the same place amongst us, making allowance for altered circumstances, as the epigram did with the Greeks.—*The Westminster Review.*

The student of poetry knows that no form of verse is a surer touchstone of mastery than this, it is so easy to write badly, so supremely difficult to write well, so full both of hindrance and of occasion in all matters of structure and style; neither any a more searching test of inspiration, since on the one hand it seems to provoke the affectations of ingenuity, and on the other hand it has been chosen by the greatest men of all as the medium for their most intimate, direct, and overwhelming self-disclosures.—*The Same.*

A sonnet is, in its highest moods, an epic in fourteen lines.—THOMAS HOOD, THE YOUNGER.

With reference to laws of structure in regular sonnets, it is self-evident, as regards the sonnet of compound stanza, that there are four different forms into which may fall a metrical structure consisting of an octave of a prescriptive arrangement of rhymes and a sestet consisting of another set of rhymes that are free in arrangement from prescription. And some years ago the present writer exemplified these in 'four sonnets on the sonnet,' one only of which, under the name of 'The Sonnet's Voice,' originally printed in the 'Athenæum,' was widely circulated in sonnet anthologies. These varieties of the sonnet of octave and sestet are: (1) The sonnet in which the stronger portion both in rhythm and substance is embodied in the sestet. (2) The sonnet in which the stronger portion both in rhythm and in substance is embodied in the octave. (3) The sonnet in which the sestet is not separated from the octave, but seems to be merely a portion of the octave's movement rising to a close more or less climacteric. (4) The sonnet in which the sestet seems to be added to the octave's movements, added after its apparent termination in a kind of tailpiece answering to what in music we call the 'coda.'—THEODORE WATTS-DUNTON.

Le sonnet est un petit poème qui semble avoir la supériorité sur toutes les autres petites pièces de poésie, à cause de l'exactitude qu'on exige dans les quatorze vers dont il est composé ; la moindre négligence passe pour un crime, et on exige, avec une élégance continue, que le sonnet soit vif et naturel.—BEAUZÉE.

As we are told that the mere obedient observance of a rule of religious life contains and unfolds high, unguessed, and mystical spiritual virtues, so the mere obedience to the metrical laws of the sonnet implies and brings with it the beauties of the 'crescendo,' the evolution of thought, the climax, the fall—the beauties more hidden and subtle than these. This necessary obedience has respect to the shape of a sonnet rather than to the rhymes. That is to say, if the divisions into quatrains and tercets, and the pauses proper to each are observed, no injury will be done to the best perfection of the sonnet by the use of a greater variety of rhymes than the Petrarchan type permits. We must remember that the Italian language has an inexhaustible source of rhymes in the regular conjugation of verbs which the English has not. Against the shape of the sonnet the greatest offence is the use of a final couplet; this, especially if isolated, as it generally is, has a quasi-epigrammatic turn ; and epigram has nothing to do with this noble form. Another common offence is the neglect of the pause at the end of the second quatrain ; and a third is the intro-

SONNET PRINCIPLES

duction of a final Alexandrine, which simply ruins the peculiar music of the sonnet.—*The Tablet.*

If it be required that the quatrains must not contain more than two rhymes, nor the tercets more than three, and that these rhymes should recur in particular places according to rule ; if no word should be introduced merely for the sake of the rhyme ; if the sonnet should develop one thought or feeling gracefully and completely, without a word too much or too little, without obscurity, irrelevancy, commonplace or extravagance ; if the major system should close in the eighth line with a full stop, and not run on into the ninth ; if in the last line the thought should reach a climax full of energy and force, or the sonnet should die away at its close like a falling sky rocket, as if from pure exhaustion of the idea which is its life ; and if in addition to these stringent conditions, it should be the unmistakeable result of poetic inspiration and fraught with sacred fire : how rarely can even the brightest and most imaginative intellect succeed in satisfying these numerous requirements !—*Saturday Review.*

Modern taste seeks in sonnets for qualities not always associated with that beautiful organism of verse. It is not that we do not recognise the value of the state and restraint of the ideal sonnet ; but taking these for granted, we desire vitality and a certain impulse. In other words, we are most delighted with a sonnet which is an organism —as we have just called it—rather than a construction. In all definite and limited forms with parts to them— and the sonnet is the only one of many such forms that English literature has retained—there must be either construction or organism—the latter word implying a certain life, a spring, a unity. A sonnet which has this quality of vitality and impetus and movement is the one perfect form and shape in English verse. All other such shapes have been discarded—shape of ballade, of rondel, of rondeau, of virelay, and so forth ; and English poetry, but for the survival of the sonnet, would be altogether

SONNET PRINCIPLES

devoted to lyrical and heroic verse which has no shape or limitation as to length, or relation of parts. Doubtless, the freedom of such verse has been excellent for English vigour; we have no wish to see our poetry bound in the too ingenious regulations of earlier Italian versification. But let the sonnet remain as long as English Letters, pure and distinct, a perfect form, and vascular and alive.—ALICE MEYNELL.

Mr. Mark Pattison tells you that 'a sonnet must consist of fourteen lines, neither more nor less'; that all 'the lines must be lines of five beats or metrical accents'; that 'as to arrangement, the lines must rime'; that 'in disposition of the rimes the whole sonnet may be regarded as composed of two systems; the first eight lines forming one system, and the remaining six the other'; while 'the first system of eight lines is composed of two quatrains,' and 'the second system of two tercets.' Mr. Pattison's next paragraph embodies the rule for rhyming the quatrains; his next, the rule for rhyming the tercets; his next, the rule for choosing the two sets of rhymes; his next, the rule which compels you so to arrange your rhymes in the tercets as 'not to reproduce the disposition of those in the quatrains'; his next, the rule against double rhymes; and his last, the rule which obliges you to refrain from rounding off your quaterzains with the clink and swagger of a couplet. This is merely the section of 'Form.' The section of 'Material' is just as complete and many-sided. It teaches you to aspire to unity as an essential quality, to 'lead up to and open' your unique thought or mood 'in the early lines of the sonnet—strictly, in the first quatrain'; and in the second quatrain to place your hearer 'in full possession of it'; to 'lay around' in a Petrarchian manner (so to speak) after the second quatrain, for the production of 'a pause, not full, nor producing the effect of a break . . . but as of one who is turning over what has been said in the mind to enforce it further.' Your next proceeding must be to

SONNET PRINCIPLES

see that 'the opening of the second system, strictly the first tercet,' is flexible enough to 'turn back upon the thought or sentiment, take it up, and carry it forward to the conclusion.' Having got so far, you must look after your conclusion, and constrain it to be 'a resultant, summing the total of the suggestion in the preceding lines,' neither more nor less than 'as a lakelet in the hills gathers into a still pool the running waters contributed by its narrow area of gradients.' Nor is this all. You are getting on, but you are not yet a perfect sonneteer. You have still to bear in mind that while your conclusion ought to 'leave a sense of finish and completeness, it is necessary to avoid anything like epigrammatic point.' You have still to note that 'by this the sonnet is distinguished from the epigram,' in which the 'conclusion is everything,' while 'in the sonnet the emphasis is nearly, but not quite, equally distributed,' inasmuch as there is 'a slight swell, or rise, about the middle.' You have still to learn to move gracefully when shackled with 'other restraints'; as that, not reckoning 'particles, auxiliaries, or familiar epithets,' you employ no word twice over, 'unless where some particular effect is aimed at by the repetition,' that, however partial you may be to 'a feeble or expletive line,' you must learn to do without them, inasmuch as they 'cannot be tolerated'; that, however closely you have modelled your style on Mr. Browning's, you must shun 'an obscure line,' as though it were a manifestation of the Principle of Evil. 'Obscurity,' Mr. Pattison remarks judiciously, 'is a fault in any writing, prose or verse;' and 'in a short poem, such as a sonnet, an obscure line is not only lost itself, it diffuses dimness over the whole piece.' The reason is that 'the intellect of the hearer has not space to recover from the perplexity into which it has been thrown,' by the obscurity in question, ' before the end of the piece is reached.'—*Saturday Review.*

Quel est donc l'imbécile qui traite si légèrement le sonnet et n'en voit pas la beauté pythagorique ? Parce que

SONNET PRINCIPLES

la forme est contraignante, l'idée jaillit plus intense. Tout va bien au sonnet; la bouffonnerie, la galanterie, la passion, la rêverie, la méditation philosophique. Il y a là la beauté du métal et du minéral bien travaillés. Avez-vous observé qu'un morceau de ciel aperçu par un soupirail, ou entre deux cheminées, deux rochers, ou par une arcade, etc., donnait une idée plus profonde de l'infini que le grand panorama vu du haut d'une montagne ? Quant aux longs poèmes, nous savons ce qu'il faut en penser ; c'est la ressource de ceux qui sont incapables d'en faire de courts. Tout ce qui dépasse la longueur de l'attention que l'être humain peut prêter à la forme poétique, n'est pas *un* poème.—*Baudelaire.*

With that profound sense of the analogies of Religion and Nature which pervades everything that Mr. Aubrey de Vere has written, he ingeniously suggests that ' the sonnet is in poetry what the Collect is in devotion.' Within the narrow limits to which its structure confines it, ' there is room at once for meditation and observation, for the imaginative and the impassioned ; and these four blended elements, far from impairing, intensify its unity.' C. W. RUSSELL, D.D.

In its solemn mood it seems as if it should be graven on marble ; yet it can be buoyant as a flower and light as a dewdrop. While enriched by rhymes, it also demands, like the Miltonic blank verse, a nobler music, varying from the simplest to the subtlest cadences of metrical harmony. It requires a diction strong, pure, felicitous, and lucid. It should end with an increased ascent and elevation, or else with a graduated dying away.—AUBREY DE VERE.

A true sonnet is characterised by greatness, not prettiness ; and, if complex in structure, it is in substance solidly simple. Its oneness is its essence. It is not a combination of many thoughts, but the development of a single thought so large as to be, latently, a poem.
THE SAME.

SONNET PRINCIPLES

Without entering into the question of the structure of these exquisite miniatures, a sonnet is a poem expressing in fourteen lines a single thought, emotion or fact, and expressing it in poetical language and by means of a natural transition which should take place in the Petrarchan sonnet at the end of its opening octave. The form is brief, but sufficient for this single purpose of a single expression ; it is, in the words of Carducci, *un breve ed amplissimo carme.*—GEORGE A. GREENE.

The sonnet is a form of poetry in which style is put under high pressure, and the wealth it contains is rarely to be won without toil. Condensation of thought, exactitude of language, and unity of design are demanded of the sonnet writer, and through his fourteen lines, and knitting them together, must run the golden thread of poetry.—JOHN DENNIS.

Archbishop Trench has well said that ' poems of the highest order are in their very essence sources of delight which is inexhaustible.' This delight is afforded in no stinted measure by the sonnet, which concentrates within a narrow space so rare and peerless beauty. A sonnet, brief though it be, is of wide compass, and contains, to use the words of Marlowe, infinite riches in a little room. What depths of emotion, what graceful fancy, what majestic organ-notes, what soft flute-like music is it not capable of expressing ?—THE SAME.

In those fourteen lines one thought, and only one, can with proper freedom and fulness of expression rise to its climax and sink to its close. There is a quasi-legend about the birth of this wonderfully perfect solitary stanza.[1] ' Upon a day Apollo met the nine Muses and the three Graces in sweet sport mixed with earnest. Memory, the grave and noble mother of the Muses, was there likewise. Each of the fourteen spoke a line of verse.

---

[1] 'A Talk about Sonnets,' *Blackwood's Magazine*, August 1880.

SONNET PRINCIPLES

Apollo began ; then each of the nine Muses sang her part ; then the three Graces warbled each in turn ; and finally a low sweet strain from Memory made a harmonious close. This was the first sonnet, and, mindful of its origin, all the poets take care to bid Apollo strike the key-note for them when they compose one, and to let Memory compress the pith and marrow of the sonnet into its last line.'—FREDERICK C. KOLBE, D.D.

The sonnet and its peculiarities, whether it should end in a point or die away like a refluent wave, has for long been a favourite exercising ground for critics. *Solvitur ambulando.* A sonnet, like an epic or a ballad, has only a right to exist when it is good as a poem, and a pocket collection would easily hold all the English sonnets which are poetry. As a rule, a bad sonnet—that is, most sonnets—tails off and expires in feebleness, the bard being exhausted in his contest with rhymes, which are ' stubborn things.' A sonnet is in poetry what a gem is in the sister art, but there are more good gems than sonnets.—*The Daily News.*

There is no undue artificiality in a sonnet as a vehicle of expression. Adequate thought or emotion, once carefully enshrined in metrical form so complex, acquires independent being. Writing a sonnet is thus the same as giving organic body to a fragmentary soul, which would else be imperceptible to sense and without duration in this world. But the very artificiality of the vehicle, the fixity of the stanza, renders it a source of strength to those who are not in a high sense creative. When they have mastered the conditions of the sonnet, they can pour into that deftly fashioned vase a liquid thought or feeling which shall afford refreshment to many generations. Such singers do not demand the elbow-room of infinity. Most of the greatest require it. Therefore the sonnet's narrow plot is an advantage for the former, an irksome limitation for the latter.—JOHN ADDINGTON SYMONDS.

SONNET PRINCIPLES

A quatrain as the unit of the base, a tercet or a couplet as the unit of the turn, in a stanza of fourteen lines, will be found to constitute the fundamental integers of every sonnet, in whatever language or however these elementary parts shall have been variously put together. Experiments in which the broad correlation of base to turn is neglected do not propagate their species, however admirable they may be as poems of fourteen irregularly rhyming verses. On the other hand, numerous subdivisions of the two authentic sonnet types, Petrarchan and Shaksperian, have been cultivated.—THE SAME.

The sonnet is no arbitrary or haphazard invention, but is based on reasonable rules, which are accepted and observed most cheerfully by the very men who are big enough to break them.—A. T. QUILLER-COUCH.

> Sonnets stiff in all their joints,
> Spurred by exclamation points.
>   ANTONY MOREHEAD.

> The sonnet, erst reserved in Ages Dark
> For songs of love by Shakspere and Petrarch,
> Is now considered fit for any theme,
> Cant, metaphysics, bricks and mortar, steam.
>   ANON.

The lawlessness which young poets demand in the name of inspiration, if it sets them free, bewilders the hearer, who does not know what to expect. The critic should remember, if the poet does not, that rhythmic effects depend jointly on the sounds uttered, and on the expectation of the ear. If there are to be no recognised rules of sonnet composition, the hearer will be defrauded of the satisfaction which comes from the recognition of a prescribed form. The composer has rescued his own spontaneity; he has forfeited the advantage of addressing a disciplined ear. To indite a sonnet, and at the same time to refuse obedience to the laws of the sonnet, is, as a thoughtful critic has said, to commit the absurdity of

SONNET PRINCIPLES

trying to have at the same time the pleasure derived from a sense of prescribed form, and the pleasure derived from a sense of freedom from prescribed form.
MARK PATTISON.

A literary Procrustes may as well be called the inventor of the couplet, the stanza, or the ode, as of the sonnet. They are all in a certain degree restraints on the writer. The bondage to which Pindar and his followers have submitted in the structure of strophe, antistrophe, and epode, is much greater than that which the sonnet imposes. If the scanty thought be disgustingly dilated, or luxuriant ideas unnaturally compressed, what follows? Not, surely, that it is impossible to write good odes or good sonnets, but that the poet was injudicious in the choice of his subject, or knew not how to adjust his metre to his thoughts.—JOHN MALONE.

The subject should, according to the strictest division, be set forth in the first and illustrated in the second quatrain; confirmed by the first tercet, and concluded in the last; and much of the excellence of a sonnet will depend upon the beauty of its close, which, without being epigrammatical, should artfully wind up the subject with some striking thought or expression.
Edinburgh Review, No. XII.

Qual cosa più agevole che il far quattordici versi, e persuadersi di aver fatto un sonetto?—TIRABOSCHI.

Le sonnet est peut-être le cercle le plus parfait qu'on ait pu donner à une grande pensée et la division la plus régulière que l'oreille ait pu lui préscrire.—MARMONTEL.

The sonnet is a form of poetry that seems made on purpose either to embody a striking thought, or a vivid impression, or an inspiring mood, or a dominant memory, and so to embody it that it brings the thought, or impression, or mood, or memory back in its fullest power to those who have been possessed by it, and so that it takes possession for the first time of those who have never been possessed by it, as if it had been their own. Such, for instance, is Blanco White's splendid sonnet on death and immortality; such are Wordsworth's on London as seen in the early morning from Westminster Bridge, and on Milton; such is Matthew Arnold's on Sophocles and Shakespeare; such is David Gray's on the longing for spring.—*The Spectator*, May 14, 1887.

Mr. Wilfrid Blunt writes the sonnet in a Shakesperian or quasi-Shakesperian form, and has the easy advantage of that great name over those who hold the Petrarchan formula to be not only the most beautiful, but the most fitted to express with dignity the intellectual act that is the cause of a sonnet. But the name, though it is the greatest in literature, is not the greatest in lyrical poetry, and its authority is quite measurable with that of others. Moreover, the fact that Shakespeare wrote strongly, or exquisitely, or thoughtfully, in a certain form, does not deny the fact that a better form existed, neglected in his time. The final couplet with its point and epigram, suited his matter admirably, as some other form, even less grave, might have suited it. None the less is the separateness of the final couplet alien from the organic unity of the highest form of the sonnet, and none the less is the snapping epigram of the final couplet alien from the meditativeness of a high sonnet's thought and from the composure of its utterance. As regards the effect to the ear, the highest beauty of the sextet is to rise in sound and to accelerate in movement towards the close, and to end in a line or a half-line of peace; and this the couplet makes impossible.
Weekly Register, November 23, 1889.

Ogni piccola colpa è vergognosa
  Dentro un sonetto, e l' uditor s' offende
  D'una rima che venga un po' ritrosa :
O se per tutto egual non si distende,
  O non è numeroso, o se la chiusa
  Da quel che sopra proporrai, non pende.

SONNET PRINCIPLES

    E altrui non val quella si magra scusa
      Di dir che troppo rigida è la legge
      Che in quattordici versi sta rinchiusa :
    E che mal si sostiene e mal si regge
      Per scarsezza di rime, e l' intelletto
      Talor quel che non piace a forza elegge.
    In questo di Procruste orrido letto
      Chi ti sforza a giacer ?   Forse in rovina
    Andrà il Parnaso senza il tuo sonetto ?
          BENEDETTO MENZINI (*died* 1704).

    Une idée qui se développe graduellement, enchassée dans les rimes pareilles et symétriquement alternées des quatrains, et qui, arrivée aux tercets, s'accélère entre des rimes nouvelles et variées, puis se dénoue à l'improviste : tel est le seul sonnet qui mérite ce nom.—A. DE GAGNAUD.

    In all the literatures of Europe the sonnet is prominent in its pathetic and rhetorical forms. It is mainly subjective and Petrarchan. Any reader who turns over the leaves of a competent selection of English, or French, or Italian sonnets must be struck with the fact that in their large majority they express the secret sentiment or emotional experience of the soul, and that even where they seem to be descriptive, they deal mainly with the effect of external phenomena on the moods of the writer. No species of poetry is more confidential than the sonnet ; none has been used, since its first invention, more persistently for the transmission of those secret thoughts which almost evade articulate expression.—EDMUND GOSSE.

    Si je m'en suis tenu au sonnet, c'est que je trouve que dans sa forme à la fois mystique et mathématique, c'est le plus beau des poèmes à forme fixe, et qu'il exige, par sa brièveté et sa difficulté, une conscience dans l'exécution et une concentration dans la pensée qui ne peuvent qu'exciter et pousser à la perfection l'artiste digne de ce beau nom.—JOSÉ-MARIA DE HEREDIA.

SONNET PRINCIPLES

When a sonnet is well conceived and well executed, there is a oneness, a completeness about it that is very satisfactory to the judicious reader. In other lyrical measures there is far more danger of diffuseness. The austerity of perfection is rare. After two stanzas the Muse is prone to go on to another and another, lest she should be suspected of being soon out of breath. But in a conscientious sonnet the eighth line already pulls you up sharply with a warning that, if you have anything very good to say, you had better say it and have done with it.

M. R.

The sonetto is a lyrical composition in rhyme, consisting of fourteen verses or lines, and each line consisting of eleven syllables—in English ten syllables, and very rarely eleven. It is composed of two quatrains and two triplets. The first eight lines, or two quatrains, admit only two rhymes or terminations of the same sound; but these may be disposed in either of two ways. According to one, which is the most common, the rhymes fall respectively as follows: one upon the first, fourth, fifth and eighth lines; and the other upon the second, third, sixth and seventh lines. According to the other arrangement, the rhymes are disposed alternately as in the usual English elegiac quatrain—that is to say, one of the two terminates on the first, third, fifth and seventh lines; and the other on the second, fourth, sixth and eighth lines. No other arrangement of the metre is admissible in the first eight lines, but each of the two forms now mentioned is used by the best writers. In the remaining six lines, composed of two *ternari* or triplets, now usually called tercets, a greater latitude is allowed. The two most regular and perfect forms are the following: in one two rhymes only are used, terminating alternately upon the first, third and fifth lines; and upon the second, fourth and sixth lines. In the other form three rhymes are admitted, terminating respectively, one upon the first and fourth lines, another upon the second and fifth lines, and another upon the third and sixth lines. But it is also allowed, and not uncommon when three rhymes are used, to dispose them among the six lines in some different order, according to the pleasure of the writer; under this limitation, only, that two lines in immediate succession do not rhyme together. More than three rhymes are in no case admissible in the two triplets. It follows from the explanation here given that the regular sonnet admits only four, or at most five, metrical terminations of different sounds.—JAMES GLASSFORD.

A mediocre sonnet is more hateful to gods and men than any other versified mediocrity, a crabbed one is harder to read than any other form of crabbed verse; and complete success is not common even when the thought is not over deep; but to express some deep piece of thought or feeling completely and with beauty in the narrow limits of fourteen lines, and in such a way that no line should be useless or barren of some reflex of the main idea; to leave the due impression of the whole thought on the mind by the weight and beauty of the ending; and to do all this without losing simplicity, without affectation of any kind, and with exquisite choiceness of diction and rhyme, is as surely a very great achievement, and among the things most worth doing, as it is exceedingly rare to find done.
WILLIAM MORRIS.

POSTSCRIPT

THE foregoing 'Sonnet Principles' have been drawn chiefly from two sources—the introductions to the numerous collections of sonnets which have been published in these later years, and the criticisms passed upon those collections.

The century which is so near its end has been a century of sonnet-anthologies, and the first century to form such a collection. The earliest is not Capel Lofft's 'Laura,' in 1813, but George Henderson's 'Petrarca,' ten years before; while the next anthologist was twenty years later—R. F. Housman in 1833, followed since by Dyce, Leigh Hunt, Tomlinson, Dennis, Main, Hall Caine, Sharp, Waddington, Quiller-Couch, and others. Each of these has prefixed a critical discussion of the history and nature of the sonnet, as Mr. Mark Pattison has done in his edition of Milton's Sonnets.

But the student of sonnet literature will perhaps derive more benefit from the reviews of these books, which the date of each publication will enable him to find in such journals as the 'Athenæum,' the 'Academy,' and the 'Spectator.' Mr. Theodore Watts-Dunton is known to have expounded his views in the first of these, as well as in the important essay on the sonnet in the ninth edition of the 'Encyclopædia Britannica;' and the reviews in the 'Academy' were in many cases signed by another name of high authority, the late J. Addington Symonds. The fortunate reader who has access to the British Museum may extend his search to the contemporary issues of the 'Tablet' and the 'Weekly Register,' in whose sonnet-papers the initiated have often detected

POSTSCRIPT

the thought and style of the gifted lady to whom my collection is dedicated. But the 'Sonnet Principles' to which I have attached her name have been taken from signed articles in 'Merry England.'

Not only the British Museum but some public libraries, such as those of Dublin, Newry, and Chicago—to name three that I chance to know—will enable the devotee of the sonnet to consult a series of papers from which (as they are my own) I should have wished to annotate the present anthology. The papers run through many volumes of the 'Irish Monthly,' the first beginning at page 335 of Vol. XIV. (1886) and embodying a very admirable little essay on the sonnet which had appeared in 1877 in a clever but short-lived journal called 'Yorick.' Other papers on my special subject begin at page 568 of Vol. XV., pp. 366 and 733 of Vol. XVI., pp. 380, 616 and 651 of Vol. XVII., page 321 of Vol. XIX., and page 442 of Vol. XX. (1891). The list might be continued.

Mr. William Sharp, in the Introduction to his delightful 'Sonnets of this Century,' has bestowed very emphatic praise on 'the anonymous contributor of two highly interesting papers on sonnet-literature which appeared in the "Dublin Review" in 1876 and 1877'; and 'Notes and Queries' of April 21, 1877, said: 'One of the best and fullest accounts of English sonnet-writers, and of foreign ones also, especially German and French, brought down to the present time, with copious specimens, will be found where no one would think of looking for it—in the "Dublin Review" of October 1876 and January 1877.' I am glad to put on record that this 'Critical History of the Sonnet,' which is certainly one of the most complete surveys of the subject that have yet appeared, was written by the Rev. Dr. C. W. Russell, President of Maynooth College (1857-1880). It was his last contribution to a Review of which he had for forty years been one of the main supports and for many years practically the editor, as may be seen in Mr. Wilfrid Ward's 'Life of Cardinal Wiseman,' and much more fully in the

POSTSCRIPT

admirable sketch of the history of the first sixty years of the 'Dublin Review' given in its own pages in April 1896 by the Rev. Dr. Casartelli.

Lavish as I have been of 'Sonnets on the Sonnet,' I have not exhausted my store. There are two for which I wish to find room at the last moment. An unknown quantity, X, in the 'Semaine Religieuse' of Viviers, 1895, thinks there can be no good sonnets north of Paris.

> Oui, j'aime le sonnet. C'est la langue immortelle
> Chère de siècle en siècle aux vrais fils d'Apollon.
> La règle, avez-vous dit, met la muse en tutelle
> Et sur l'Art fait peser une chape de plomb.
> Mais on sculpte le marbre et non pas le moëllon :
> Des pensers vagabonds, de la forme rebelle,
> Coulés en son métal sort une œuvre plus belle.
> S'il est mauvais parfois, du moins il n'est pas long.
>
> Jumeau de l'olivier, depuis l'Andalousie
> Jusqu'aux Alpes, du Rhône aux côteaux florentins,
> Il prospère au soleil des rivages latins ;
> Mais son cristal où brille une liqueur choisie,
> Vermeille ou couleur d'or, se brise dans la main
> Trop lourde du Saxon, du Scythe, et du Germain.

Joseph Autran (1813-1877) was an Academician and poet of note : he may, therefore, close my long series of the Sonnet's Laureates :

> Je t'invoque, Sonnet ! Fi du poëme énorme
> Qui de ses douze chants assomme l'auditeur !
> Sur le ton solennel que tout autre endorme,
> Toi, tu n'as pas le temps d'assoupir un lecteur.
>
> J'aime ton pas léger, j'aime ta mince forme,
> Ayant si peu de corps, tu n'as pas de lenteur.
> On fait un lourd fagot avec le bois d'un orme,
> Avec un brin de rose on fait une senteur.
>
> Va donc, cours et reviens ; demande à l'hirondelle
> Cet essor qui franchit tout le ciel d'un coup d'aile ;
> Au fier cheval de Job emprunte son galop.
>
> Sois l'éclair, le rayon, le regard, le sourire ;
> Sonnet ! fais en un mot que l'on ne puisse dire :
>   'Quatorze vers, c'est encor trop !'

POSTSCRIPT

At page 55 of this book the once famous Corn Law Rhymer, Ebenezer Elliot (whom one is surprised to find in such company) speaks of a certain completely forgotten sonneteer, Fitzadam, in the same breath with Milton and Wordsworth. There are two or three of Fitzadam's sonnets in Mr. R. F. Housman's collection; but he is ignored in all later anthologies.

This half-century, as I have remarked, has produced many anthologies. Perhaps this anthology of 'Sonnets on the Sonnet' is the last of them till the twentieth century begins. Though more confined in its scope than the others, I trust that it will be found to possess a value and interest of its own. The kind reader will at least refrain from dismissing my poets with those rude words of old Thomas Nashe: 'Put out your rush-lights, ye rimers, and bequeath your crazed quaterzayns to the chaundlery.'

COLOPHON

All sonnets, all about the Sonnet!
A sonnet-theme, in form a sonnet.
   What other mould of poet's art
   Were fit to play this double part,
Or have a book like this writ on it?

INDEX OF AUTHORS

ADAMSON, 16
Alexander, 8
Anonymous, 14, 15, 16, 18, 20, 40, 54, 117
Auld, 35, 36, 61
Autran, 117

BARRY, ALICE, 73
Baudin, 44
Bayley, 54
Blanchemain, 66
Blunt, Wilfrid, 26
Boileau, 2
Boulmier, 91
Boursault, 47
Bowker, 92
Brizeux, 62
Brownlow, 66, 74, 89

CARDUCCI, 64, 65
Cochrane, 39
Cole, 40
Coleridge, 99
Collier, 4
Creamer, 32

DEANE, 31, 97
Desmarais, 5
De Vigny, 68
Dobson, 87
Dorr, Julia, 34

EARLE, 58
Edmeston, 37
Edwards, 6
Elliot, 55, 56

FABER, 28
Fitzgerald, 9
Forshaw, 74
Francis, M. E., 72

GARNIER, 46
Gaut, 48
Gautier, 10
Gibson, 5
Gilder, 33, 60
Gladstone, W. E., 19
Goethe, 42
Greene, 9

HAMILTON, EUGENE LEE, 50, 60
Hamilton, Sir Wm. Rowan, 17
Haskin, 38
Henley, 90, 96
Henry, 83
Hipp, 47
Hurtado de Mendoza, 3

JUDKIN, 14

KANE, 75
Kappey, 36

INDEX OF AUTHORS

Keating, 83
Keats, 25
Kolbe, 73

La Coste, 43
Lafond, 67
Lang, 52
Loeben, 13
Lofft, 24
Longfellow, 99
Lowell, 22, 70
Luders, 95

Macdonald, George, 86
Macdonald, Mosse, 71
McKeon, 59
Magnier, 44
Mason, 49
Meilhac, 11
Méray, 67
Montagu, 15
Morehead, 7
Motte, de la, 19

New, 28
Noble, 33
Norcross, 77

O'Brien, Charlotte, 64, 65, 76
O'Connor, 10, 75
O'Neill, 42, 62, 68

Perry, 29
Platen, 63
Plunkett, 72
Poe, 39
Prati, 49

Robinson, A. M. F., 20
Robinson, Harriet, 17

Rossetti, 25
Roux, 45
Russell, 3, 6, 12, 78-82, 88, 97

St-Amand, 96
Sainte-Beuve, 53
Schiebeler, 13
Schiller, 98
Schlegel, 12
Scollard, 94
Scott, W. B., 27
Seward, 6, 23
Sherman, 98
Shoemaker, 41, 56, 58
Skeat, 91
Soulary, 46
Stephen, 27
Stewart, 93
Stock, 37
Sweetman, 71
Swinburne, 93
Symonds, 29

Thomas, Edith, 7
Tomlinson, 59

Upward, 38

Vaucelle, 48
Vega, Lope de, 4
Veuillot, 11, 43
Voiture, 87

Warburton, 76
Warden, 55
Watts-Dunton, 26
Wharton, Edith, 61
White, Kirke, 24
Wordsworth, 23, 53
Wright, T. H., 78, 98

www.ingramcontent.com/pod-product-compliance
Lightning Source LLC
Chambersburg PA
CBHW031333160426
43196CB00007B/674